How A
MAN
Prays for
His Family

FAMILYLIFE™
Publishing

John Yates

How a Man Prays for His Family
Author: John Yates

Published by FamilyLife Publishing, a division of Campus Crusade for Christ.
Copyright © 2004, 2005 John Yates. All rights reserved.

Formerly published—Copyright ©1996 Bethany House Publishers

Project Coordinator: Betty Rogers
Cover Copy: Dale Walters
Graphic Designer: Jennifer I. Smith
Cover Design: Jennifer I. Smith

PRINTED IN THE UNITED STATES OF AMERICA.

ISBN 1572296526

FAMILYLIFE™
Bringing Timeless Principles Home

Dennis Rainey, President
5800 Ranch Drive . Little Rock, AR 72223
(501) 223-8663 . 1-800-FL-TODAY (1-800-358-6329)
www.familylife.com

A division of Campus Crusade for Christ

contents

dedication

To John William Yates, III, Christopher Stanway Yates,
and William Steve Gaskins, the three most important
young men in my life.

acknowledgment

I am deeply grateful to my assistant, Debbie Apoldo,
whose unfailing good humor and patience made all the difference
in seeing this book completed.

foreword

For Men Who Care About Their Families

It was a Tuesday night at Veteran's Stadium in Philadelphia. Mike Schmidt threw out the ceremonial first ball for the 67th All-Star game. The man on the receiving end of that pitch was the leading vote getter for the National League team. This young man, playing in his fourth All-Star game, may one day be seen as the greatest catcher in baseball history. His name is Mike Piazza. In his first appearance at bat, he smashed the ball 445 feet for a home run. In his next plate appearance, he blasted a double off the right field wall. Halfway through the season Piazza was hitting .363 with 24 homers and 63 RBIs. People were wondering if somehow a catcher could win a Triple Crown. For Mike it was just a typical season—but the truth about how he has achieved so much is a story that greatly inspires me as a father.

Not blessed with an abundance of natural talent or speed, Mike had little to commend himself to the professional baseball draft of 1988. Only after 1,388 other players had been picked did Tommy LaSorda decide, out of the goodness of his heart, to give this son of an old friend a chance. The Dodgers felt that the kid might not have the ability, but he had worked hard, and so they drafted him as a number 62 pick. It was one of the best decisions LaSorda ever made.

By all accounts, the reason Piazza has done so well is wrapped up in his relationship with his father. Vince Piazza had an over-whelming love for the game and for his son. Neither Vince nor his son was bursting with talent, but he said, "I always dreamed of being a Major League player. I prayed to God that one of my sons would fulfill my dream."

Some contemporary child-rearing experts might disagree with this kind of approach, but Mike has always been grateful for a dad who loved him, had great faith in him, sacrificed on his behalf, coached him, and *prayed and prayed for him to succeed.*

This book is for the dads who love their children, who want to do everything they possibly can to help them develop and mature into fine young men and women. And it's for men who know that they need God's help in achieving this goal and men who want to learn how to pray effectively for their families but aren't sure how.

Sometimes it takes another man to help us grow in our relationship with God. All of my life I've been surrounded by varieties of men. For the last several years, I have met regularly, through our church's men's fellowship, with several hundred men who have shared with me a common desire to learn what it means to be a man fully alive and mature as God meant us to be. Not all of these male influences were godly, of course, but cumulatively they have helped me understand men as a whole—what motivates us, where some of our blind spots lie, our shared desires for our families, our questions about God. And so this book grows out of all these relationships and out of my experience as a husband and a father.

Most especially, I want to encourage men who are working hard to provide for their families to the best of their ability and men who realize that a family needs spiritual leadership *as well as* material provision. These men want to do the very best they can for their families and know they need God's help in the process. The goal of this book is to help men learn to find God's assistance and guidance through prayer.

We know that being a husband and a father in America at the outset of the 21st century is a great challenge. My wife and I have five grown children. For almost 30 years my family and I have lived in the Washington, D.C., area, where life is particularly pressured and frenetic, and where we take life pretty seriously. The cost of living is high and the pace of living exacts its toll on people's lives. We have not escaped the pressures of life here, by any means.

A lesson learned in the midst of some pressure will help put into perspective just where we are headed in this book. When we moved to Washington, it became obvious that owning a home in this area was beyond our reach financially. We were grateful that an adequate home was provided for us by the church where I worked. But we wanted to build equity in a house, and we hit on the idea of buying a small farmhouse in the mountains as a vacation home and place of retreat. In retrospect, it was a good decision, as it has proven to be an invaluable help to us and to the many others who have used it. But it was a decision we made slowly, carefully, and after a lot of prayer.

My wife, Susan, and I compiled a list of the things we felt were essential (such as cost and location), and other things that we would *like* but were not absolutely necessary (such as a fireplace and lots of pasture with a stream running through it). This list of specific items became our shared prayer list, and we prayed daily that we would be able to find just the right place. Eventually we did. It's a small cottage on a knoll in the foothills of the Blue Ridge Mountains, just one hour from home, located right up against the George Washington National Forest, with 10 acres that include a small stable, good pasture land, and a pond fed by a mountain stream. In fact, 12 of the 13 items that we had been praying for were provided. (I'll tell you about the 13th item in chapter 5.)

But here's the point I'm coming to. Over the years I came to realize that there had been one other thing we really *needed*, yet we hadn't had the foresight to pray for it. God provided for us what we didn't know enough to ask for on our own. His name is Albert.

Albert is the man who sold us the farmhouse. He had lived there himself for 20 years, but had decided it was time to build a smaller, simpler, and easier-to-care-for place next door. Albert is in his 80's now, and he and his wife, Camille, have been married 60 years. He's a wiry little man with snow-white hair, clear, sparkling eyes, a great sense of humor, and an infectious love for people. As I said, when we were asking God to give us a place in the country, we thought we knew exactly what we needed—but we had no idea how important it would be for us to have someone like Albert, because he has the know-how to do *anything*.

As needs have arisen over the years, one by one Albert has introduced me to the people I needed to help with repairs, mowing, veterinary needs—you name it. He has rescued me over and over, whether helping me repair an old tractor or pulling me out of the mud or snow. We've been through sad times together, too, such as the death of his daughter. He has advised me in difficult situations in my work, and we must have consumed at least 500 donuts over coffee together these past years. Albert has become one of my very best friends, a man who's always available to help me during times of need.

When I was praying for a farm for my family, an investment for our future, I didn't know how much I needed an Albert. Naively, or proudly, I was sure I could handle life on my own. But I could never have managed to oversee the farm—and other parts of my life—without him. I needed a person who had walked the path of life ahead of me to show me the way. *God knew this even though I didn't, and He gave me more than I asked for when I prayed.*

We Need a God Who Sees the Road Ahead

Maybe my experience illustrates a principle that is true for most men. As young men, we imagine we can handle things on our own, but as we get older we realize how much we need help. The fortunate men wake up and realize how much they need God's help, as well. Even more than we need older men like Albert, we each need our heavenly Father's direction and care. Many men fail to understand this until they have lived a few years and grappled with life and the responsibilities that come with being a man, a husband, and a father.

Then, somewhere during the middle years of manhood, a transition occurs in a man's attitudes. As young men, many of us were concerned with sex and success. If you're a follower of Christ, and if you've heard the biblical teachings on the husband's leadership in the home, this may feed your sense of responsibility to be the leader, to have the right answers, to provide for and protect your family. But as time passes, our awareness of life begins to broaden. For example, if a man succeeds in his career, then success no longer is enough and he begins to think about *significance*, about his desire to make his life count, to make a difference. If he has not hit the career goals he'd hoped for, that pain often has a way of forcing him to ask similar questions: What really is important in my life? What things matter most for me?

> *Begin to think about significance, not just success.*

And then there are these other people in our lives—our wives and children. As the children grow, we become more aware of their great needs and how difficult it is to be the father they deserve. Fathering is a lot more complicated than just having children. Very quickly, children begin to teach a man about his own limitations, that he doesn't have all the answers, and that he frequently fails as a husband and a dad. I do not know a man for whom futility and failure does not cause pain. It's frightening when your child is seriously ill and you've done all you can do. It's frustrating when you have tried your best to control one of your "out of control" kids and failed. When someone you love is facing problems you don't know how to fix, it hurts. And yet it's this sense of inadequacy that helps us to realize how much we need God's help.

This is the beginning of a whole new way of life called prayer.

The young man often makes the mistake of thinking that he must always be right. But the wise man learns, in time, that headship means taking responsibility to see that your wife and children have all that they need. Because we cannot provide all that they need—or even *know* all their real needs—prayer is our best resource.

Many books have been published lately about the man's roles and responsibilities at home. This book is about our calling as servant-leaders at home—particularly *to pray for our families*. We are called to provide and support in very practical ways; it's true. But none is more important than to seek and find the loving guidance, warning, course correction, and comfort we can receive for our families as we learn to hear from our heavenly Father.

In the Old Testament book of Judges, there is a strange story about a man named Micah who wanted to provide a religious influence for his home. He went out and located a young priest whom he hired and brought home to live with his family. This man was to be the family's personal priest or minister, but it didn't work. It backfired, and the result was great loss and sadness for the whole family. You can't hire someone else to be the priest for your family. The minister or the youth pastor of your church can't be the primary man of God for your children. The father has to take on that role for his family. In the simplest sense, a priest is someone who tries to bring God to His people and then, in turn, represents His people before God. In the Old Testament a priest was a sort of mediator between God and man. Christ became our mediator with God, and the New Testament teaches that now all who follow Him have a role as priests to the unbelieving world (1 Peter 2:9). As Christians, we have the responsibility to serve as "priests" in our day—that means, simply, representing God to others and representing others to God in prayer.

This is particularly important in the case of the husband and father with his family. *The father is to be God's representative to his wife and children.* He has the opportunity to bring God to them, which means showing his family what

God is like through word and deed. Similarly, he has the responsibility to bring them to God by showing them how to become followers of Christ, listening for God's direction, and caring for them throughout their lives. It's a big responsibility, but an even bigger privilege. A man who loves his family will pray for them. But for most men, prayer doesn't come easily—particularly for a busy man. And so we'll take some time to examine the questions and practical roadblocks that trip us up, make us quit before we start, or leave us wondering if prayer is only talking to the ceiling. I hope you'll find answers and practical help here, too.

God has entrusted a wife and children into our care. We can know the power and work of God in their lives. And we can deepen our own relationship with God in ways that will transform us, when we learn the walk and the dialogue known to us as prayer.

I'm Not Sure I'm Cut Out for Prayer 1

Richard had spent the better part of the weekend helping me replace the rotten dock in our pond. Because he is an engineer and exceptionally good with carpentry projects, I had eagerly accepted his offer of some help.

I'd known Richard slightly for a couple of years, but that weekend I got to know him much better. It was a difficult time in his life because he had just learned his full-time job as a consultant was to be ended. In his early 50's, and not blessed with great financial resources, this was a huge blow for him. Richard was a new believer in Christ. As he described for me the underlying reasons for his difficulties at work, I realized that he was in crisis. Before we completely finished the dock, we talked about the need to pray for God's help in his job search. We both began to pray that God would give him the work he needed.

This was a big step for Richard. Talking to God about such concrete needs had never been a normal part of his experience.

That was years ago. Recently, Richard and his wife, Audrey, were with us for dinner, and they talked exuberantly about the amazing way in which, ever since that time, Richard has always had work. Some time after the full-time job finished, and after we began to pray, he was offered part-time work as a consultant with the same company. The company has continued to need his services ever since, and a few years ago he was taken back on as a full-time consultant. There has never been a period of more than a few weeks when he wasn't consulting with them at a good salary, doing the same work he'd always done.

As we talked, Richard and Audrey marveled that the family's needs had always been met, and that Richard had deepened in his faith through being placed in a position where he has had to trust daily in God. He has found his prayers answered in unexpected ways, and he's always had everything he's needed. But more than that, the lack of long-term security has, in actual fact, taught him to entrust his future to God and trained him to become a man of faith, courage, and prayer.

Like Richard, many of us men are in the process of learning how to trust God and how to pray. But these lessons rarely come easy. For most of us, learning to pray takes some time, involves getting some advice, and grows out of some urgency in our lives. This is particularly true of another friend, whom I'll call Matt.

> *In order to be a whole man, it's as important to be growing spiritually as it is to be maturing physically and intellectually.*

Six or seven of us were gathered around a table in a high-rise office in downtown Washington, D.C. We'd been meeting for a year and a half, whenever our crowded schedules would allow, to talk about what it means in a man's life when he begins to think seriously about his own relationship with God. Light was streaming in from a dramatic summer sunset as we looked down across the Potomac River to the Kennedy Center. From a Washington perspective, I was in the midst of a "power" group: three enormously successful corporate presidents, two nationally known political commentators, and an eminent attorney. Spiritually speaking, we had come from diverse places.

That evening, our conversation went long and, finally, about 10 p.m., I suggested we call it quits. But as everyone rose to leave, Matt suggested that we pray. Now this man—who is on a first-name basis with every political power broker in the city, whose political opinions are eagerly sought left and right—led us in this prayer. "Dear God, we know that prayer works, and so we come to you asking your help...." He then prayed for us, for his family, and for some of the troubling situations we'd discussed.

It was his eagerness to pray that struck me deeply, because Matt is not a man who is known for being religious. Not long before, he wasn't even sure about the idea of men meeting "to talk about God." But on that night, it was obvious that meeting with a small group of men who are all seeking to know God better had touched him. Like us, he was being changed.

Matt's growing confidence that God hears and answers prayer is the sort of quiet miracle of personal change that is happening all over our country … and around the world.

A Spiritual Movement Among Men

Today, we're seeing amazing spiritual developments among men. Men are turning to God. We are meeting in small groups to learn more about God and to grow spiritually. We are crowding into churches and meetings aimed at spiritual growth more than I can ever remember. We are sensing a hunger for God and concluding that in order to be a whole man, it's as important to be growing spiritually as it is to be maturing physically and intellectually.

Women have understood this far better than men. We tend to be reticent about our faith. One single man told me about his girlfriend's reaction when he—at last—talked with her about the importance of his faith. He was a little bit embarrassed, not knowing how she would react since he hadn't talked much about faith before. But her response was, "I like it. It's very important to me that you have a strong faith in God." This is more typical of women than most men would expect.

You may have attended seminars aimed at personal growth. Most of us have been to workshops on time management, or on building a better marriage, or on how to be better stewards of our money. But a man's relationship with God is more important because it affects all of these areas of his life and more—and prayer is at the heart of this relationship because it is our lifeline to God Himself.

Prayer Isn't Easy

Given the importance of knowing and dialoguing with God, one big problem men face is a lack of confidence in our relationship with Him. Many of us find prayer difficult. We may even think that prayer is important, but still hard to do. It's awkward. And we have important questions about prayer:

- Is prayer real?
- Does God really hear?
- What good does prayer do?
- Why ask God to do something He may want me to do for myself?
- How many times do I ask?
- How long before answers come?
- What if my life is a mess?

Most of us have not had models for what an authentic, manly prayer life looks like. Religious people—especially ministers—pray at church, and the prayers prayed in church are beautiful. But most of us find that sort of prayer does not come easily. Women seem to pray more easily than we do. They're good at organizing prayer groups. They talk about prayer more easily. In fact, your wife may be the initiator in your home, the one who prays with the kids because it just seems to come more naturally to her. But to whom do we look?

Not long ago my sons and I had the opportunity to spend a vacation together alone in the Rocky Mountains. After several days in a rustic cabin at 10,000 feet, where we had few modern conveniences, we moved to a friend's condominium in one of the ski villages in central Colorado, where we actually had hot water and a television. During the few days we spent in these luxurious quarters, we watched some videos. We saw "Apollo 13", "Tombstone", "The Shawshank Redemption", and "The Shootist" with John Wayne. Great men's movies! But not once did I see a man praying in any of these films. Every once in a while, we see football players go down on one knee in the end zone and it looks like they're praying, but this is not particularly inspirational for the rest of us.

The truth is, as men, we're given a double message. We hear sermons and stories about it. We read the Bible and see that all the great men and women were clearly people of prayer. History is full of examples of great men and women who prayed. But most of us haven't known many men of prayer— and my personal opinion, from years in seminary and in the ministry is that most professional Christian leaders truly struggle with prayer, too.

Why Prayer Is Awkward for Most of Us

The bottom line: prayer is confusing, and foreign to the way many of us think and live. Why is that?

1ST PRAYER ISN'T OBJECTIVE. It's hard to get your hands around prayer. It's hard to know if you're really praying or just thinking, or if you're getting it right.

2ND PRAYER CAN BE FRUSTRATING. A friend of mine says that prayer is like trying to run a road race after a hurricane— everywhere you go, something seems to block your way! There are so many demands on our time, so many activities that seem important. When it comes to prayer, we have good intentions and may even start out all right. But then we get interrupted—the phone rings, or we remember something that we have to do right away. We say we'll pray later. After enough of these put-offs we can feel guilty, or think that trying to pray is useless. Sooner or later, we wonder if we're really cut out for prayer after all.

3RD IT CAN BE SO HARD TO FOCUS. For years I tried to pray in my car. I'd drive down the road, shut off the radio, and start trying to concentrate on praying. As often as not, I'd decide I needed a cup of coffee ... or start thinking about something Susan had said. Then I'd catch myself and begin to pray again ... only to find myself thinking about a particular problem I was having with someone at church. After many years, I finally gave up trying to pray in the car. My wife, on the other hand, finds it easy to pray in the car. It seems to work well for her, except for the one time when she was driving in the late afternoon in bumper-to-bumper traffic and unconsciously closed her eyes in prayer and rammed into the car in front of her!

4TH PRAYER IS, IN PART, ADMITTING OUR NEED FOR HELP—and here we step into a bind. Few men I know like to admit that they need help—even though we're confronted every day with our inadequacies (which is particularly true if you have a family). There's so much we need to know. I saw a book the other day entitled *What Men Understand About Women*, and when I opened it up, every page was blank! I don't know about you, but I have often felt that way—that I really don't know very much about raising my children, relating to my wife, or exercising my responsibility as a husband and father. We want to be the best fathers we can be. We want to provide for our children. We want to help them make the best decisions possible. We want to protect our children, to prepare them for successful adulthood, to warn them of the problems they will encounter, and to show them the right way. We want them to have good health, to get a good education, and to mature as men and women of faith, integrity, courage, compassion, and discipline. In the face of all these needs—if we stop to face them at all—we can begin to feel overwhelmed by our inability to make a difference. For instance, take the whole challenge of communicating with your kids. A friend of mine was shaving on a Saturday morning recently, and his 3-year-old was lying on his back on the bathroom rug. The little boy asked him, "Dad, what do you do, anyway?" Encouraged by his son's sudden interest in his work, my friend began to expound enthusiastically upon what he did. Finally, he looked at his son and said, "You know, it might be fun if you went to work with me one day and then you could really see what I do. Would you like that?" His son, who at that moment was focusing intently on the bathroom scale, answered by saying, "Dad, how much does this house weigh?" He had been totally oblivious to what his dad had been telling him!

Sometimes it can seem as though conversation with your wife or teenager is just as nonproductive.

And that's just on the communication side of things. Life is wonderfully complex—and challenging. Frankly, as your kids get older, you realize more and more how much you need God's help to raise them and to guide them toward maturity. We don't know nearly as much as we think we know. Perhaps your daughter is spending time with the wrong kind of friends. A young son may be sullen and refuse to respond. Another child is not studying—or not learning, anyway. In the meantime, you're thinking about the importance of SAT scores, or about all the lessons your kids have to learn before they can make a good marriage. You can tell your child what's right and how they have to live and even share with them the hard lessons you've learned. But a wise man realizes how very much he needs God's help in the whole process of being a parent.

We also know about all the other problems in our own lives—the "iffyness" of our own job, for instance, or the fact that the transmission on the car may go any day, squeezing our budget to the max. We know all too well the possibility of not having enough money to pay for a child's college tuition. We know about health problems that Mom has that we don't really want the kids to worry about. An enormous amount of life is uncertain. The older a man gets, the more he realizes that it's just not possible to have all the wisdom or resources he needs to fully provide for his children, or to completely prepare his children for the uncertainty of life itself. A man in the environmental field said the other day that this may be the last generation in which kids can safely play outdoors. A statement like that gets your attention!

Many men I know are quietly despairing about their families. A man's relationship with his wife may be in trouble. A child may have a serious illness or disability, or may be in open rebellion. His parents may be getting older and struggling with bad health. He may be looking at years of college tuition or years of nursing home bills. He may have a sibling whom he has to bail out of trouble time and again. The point is that most of us have large challenges in our families.

Ironically, it is this sense of failure and great need—our sense of being overwhelmed by so much responsibility—that can actually be the starting point of a genuine intimacy with God in prayer.

It's Need, Not Knowledge, That Matters

One of the most encouraging things Jesus said comes from the only long sermon recorded in the Gospels, the one we call the Sermon on the Mount. *Blessed are the poor in spirit, for theirs is the kingdom of heaven* (Matthew 5:3, KJV). The text means how blest are those who know their need of God. That thought gives me a great sense of relief—because if there is one thing I'm sure of, it's my need of God. Jesus was saying that is the starting place to becoming the man God wants me to become.

He talks in this sermon about the "blessed" man. He says there is a kind of relationship with God that, if we have it, we will be blessed, trusting God to give us what we need.

The word Jesus used that is translated "blessed" has several meanings. It means *happy, good, satisfied,* or *approved by God.* The same word, for instance, has been used throughout history to describe a very special island in the Mediterranean—Cyprus. It's been called the "blessed isle" because the person who lives there never needs to go anywhere else: It has natural beauty, resources, wonderful climate, fruits and flowers. It is thought that a person living there has all he could ever need or want.

Jesus, the Son of God, is saying that we can actually experience something of that sort of blessedness here in this life. We men who have such a heavy sense of responsibility weighing upon us can find release from the ultimate pressure to "make it all happen." We can begin, instead, to relax and trust God for all that we and our families need.

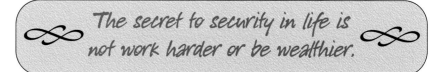

The secret to security in life is not work harder or be wealthier.

No, the secret to peace, power, and security in life is not to become omnicompetent, or simply to study and work harder, or to be more and more responsible. Neither is it to be better organized, brighter, stronger, or wealthier. Actually, the first step described by the Son of God in becoming complete and competent for the responsibilities we have is to stop relying on our own resourcefulness and recognize our great need of a powerful God! Literally, what Jesus said is, "Blessed are the poor in spirit, for theirs is the kingdom of God." In other words, those men who realize how small their personal resources are, and who turn to God out of this great sense of need, have taken the first step toward gaining all that they need to fulfill their responsibilities in life.

A man who is going to grow in relationship with God, first needs to learn how to have genuine, intimate communion with Him. This communion is the heart and soul of prayer. Power in prayer does not come from "getting it right"—that is, using the right technique, words, or system. It begins with the realization of just how inadequate we really are and that God is the only adequate One.

So if you think you're not "cut out" for prayer, you're in good company. All that is required is you and your need!

My favorite story of prayer in the New Testament comes in the account of Peter trying to walk on water to meet the Lord. His prayer wasn't eloquent or long or theologically deep. It was just real. When he started to sink, he yelled, "Lord, help me!"—and the Lord answered his cry. Peter knew his need.

On the one hand, prayer is based on a deep mystery. That mystery is how an eternal God can desire friendship and intimacy with willful men like me. But on the other hand, prayer is simple: It is lifting up to God those areas of life where we are inadequate to do the job, seeking His help from the heart.

Me, a Man of Prayer?

You can become a man of prayer. You can mature and develop into a man who truly experiences genuine communion with God. You can see God actually at work in your life. You may never get all the answers to your questions about prayer, but you can become a man of prayer—a man who talks to God on behalf of his family. And in the lives of your wife and children, that will make all the difference in the world.

For Thought and Discussion

1. What are two or three reasons you want to learn more about prayer?

2. What are your most persistent questions about prayer?

3. Is there a particular concern in your family now for which you feel you should be praying? What is it? Perhaps it would be helpful to turn these things into a simple, personal prayer to God, now, asking that the time you spend in this book or in discussion with other men will help you to deal with these concerns.

When Men Pray 2

What does it mean to be a man?

I believe that a man is fully a man only to the degree to which he is growing into the sort of person God created him to be. A man may accomplish all sorts of achievements, but if they are not pleasing to his Maker, he fails and falls short of his true potential. At the heart of true masculinity as God intended it is a relationship with Him. Unless you and I are rightly related to God and growing in our ability to be receptive to God's guidance, we are incomplete.

I remember a billboard in Raleigh, N.C., that I used to see as a boy. It said, "A man never stands so tall as when he kneels to help a boy." True enough. But we could amend this to say that a man never stands so tall as when he kneels to pray to God.

Men, we were created by God—we were not an accident. God gave us the gift of life. He breathed breath into us. But God is not like a clockmaker who builds and then leaves his work to wind down. We were made, among other things, for an ongoing, daily relationship with Him.

In Dostoyevsky's novel, *The Brothers Karamazov*, the older brother comes to visit the younger. During his visit, he mocks his younger brother's habit of kneeling at his bedside in the evening and praying. "I didn't know you still did that," says the elder brother with a sneer—implying that prayer is only for children.

Not true.

I'm grateful for the indelible image I have of my dad on his knees at bedtime. He was my model for manhood. He was strong, wise, good, hard-working, a leader in the community, faithful, responsible, well-liked, successful in his chosen work—but the heart of his life was a desire to please and to know God. He was a man of prayer, so I've wanted to be a man of prayer myself, but it has not been easy. I noticed years ago that men who struck me as being significantly effective men of God were also men particularly committed to prayer. I started getting serious about following their example when I was about 18, and I have spent more than 30 years seeking to make prayer a priority. I've prayed thoughtfully and kept written records of many prayers. I've found it instructive to recall these prayers by looking at the notes I've kept since college days. The cumulative effect of seeing so many prayers answered for more than 30 years in my own life has convinced me beyond doubt that God hears and answers prayer. I learned the maxim long ago: "Pray last—fail fast. Be smart; pray at the start."

Still, I often forget this because, like so many men, I'm tempted to act first and only later ask for God's guidance. Before we act, we need to learn to hesitate and, in that moment, seek God.

Previously, we saw that the first step toward learning to pray is recognizing our need for God. There are three other basic truths about prayer that need to be made clear here at the start:

1. Prayer won't become normal to you unless you set aside a time to pray

2. Prayer can be brief, simple, and honest

3. Prayer can become more real to us the more we practice it and the more we mature

Set Aside a Time

In Psalm 46:10 we read, *Be still, and know that I am God* (NIV).

For many of us, it's hard to be still. But when we learn to stop doing other things, we can indeed learn how to come into God's presence. God, of course, is in all places, but *we* need to be somewhere where we can be still enough to recognize His presence.

The attitude that gets us ready to pray is like the attitude we take on when coming into the presence of a truly great person. Whom do you consider to be great? As you think about the truly great people of our day, you realize that you certainly would not approach any of these people casually, or half-alert. You'd plan your meeting well. The same is true as we prepare ourselves to meet with God.

I know that everyone is different, but I've found over the years that I don't pray well in the morning until I've exercised, showered, shaved, and begun a cup of coffee. Then I feel *focused*, which is what I need to help me become still as I sit in a little room where I can be by myself. It's always in the same place and usually about the same time, which is before the rest of the family arises. Reminding myself that this is the most important moment of the day, I offer myself to God. (Later on, we'll speak about the "how" of prayer, but for now let's concentrate on the initial *attitude* of prayer.) Then I remind myself to be still. Be quiet. Be humble. That is, to be open to any direction He might give me. It's a willingness to let His will be done, so that I can truly be one with Him.

You see, if you're in harmony with God, in union and accord with Him, then you can face anything. If you've committed all things to God, then you can go forth with peace. You can trust Him—no matter what.

There are three men whose lives of prayer are an encouragement to me. Their examples in the area of prayer are quite instructive. Two are probably known to everyone reading this book, while the other is a man little known to most folks. The first, George Washington, demonstrates this first point—the importance of setting aside time for prayer.

George Washington's Example

George Washington was not only the father of our country, but also the man responsible for building the church in northern Virginia where I serve. Many historians describe him as a *deist*—a man who believed in God, but not in Jesus Christ. However, from the research I've done, it seems clear to me that Washington was not just a believer in God, but a sincere believer in Jesus as well.[1]

Washington lived an immensely disciplined life, whether on the field of battle or at home on the farm. Family records tell us that he retired every night at the same time. He would take his candle promptly at 9:00 and shut himself in his study. Few people knew what he did there, but a nephew who lived with him for 20 years became curious one night. Shortly after his uncle had entered the study, the nephew quietly opened the door and found Washington kneeling before a chair. On the chair was an open Bible. And from 9:00 until 10:00 every night, with great punctuality, he prayed and read the Word of God. Likewise, whenever he was at home, he would arise at 4:00 in the morning and return to the same study to pray and read. Even when he was fighting the Revolutionary War, he'd call his soldiers together every morning for prayer. Some of the men who served with him related that during more than one unannounced visit to Washington's tent, the general had been found on his knees in prayer. A man from France who was visiting the Continental Congress didn't know whom Washington was, and was told, "He's the one on his knees when the session goes to prayer."

Washington brought a sense of personal reverence and an attitude of humility to those halls of power. Obviously, he learned the importance of setting aside a time and place to communicate with God.

Perhaps the most personal collections of all of Washington's writings are found in a little diary of prayers that he kept. He started them when he was 20 years old and called them his "daily sacrifice." These prayers reveal a good deal about this intensely private man. How does a man who demonstrated such exceptional strength, and who carried such demands of leadership, talk with God? Notice Washington's own words carefully:

> *Pardon, I beseech Thee, my sins. Remove them from Thy presence, as far as the East is from the West.*

Did he ask this on the basis of his own character? Did he say, "Accept me, O God, for the wonder of my character, which is the marvel of all the world"? No, he said,

> *Accept me on the merits of Thy Son, Jesus Christ. I have called on Thee for pardon and forgiveness of my sins----but so coldly and carelessly that my prayers have become my sin. I stand in need of pardon. I have heard Thy Holy Word----but with such deadness of spirit that I may have been an unprofitable and forgetful hearer....*
>
> *Cover my sins with that absolute obedience of Thy dear Son, that those sacrifices which I have offered may be acceptable to Thee, in and for the sake of the sacrifice of Jesus Christ upon the cross for me. Direct my thoughts, words, and work. Wash away my sins in the immaculate blood of the Lamb and purge my heart by thy Holy Spirit from the dross of my natural corruption. Increase my faith in the sweet promises of the Gospel.*

Surely if this man who carried the weight of the young nation of America upon his shoulders followed the practice of setting aside a time and place for prayer each day, I can do the same.

The second basic truth about prayer is that prayers can be brief, simple, and honest. They need not be as eloquent as Washington's were. It was a man named Alf Stanway who taught me this truth without ever saying it in so many words.

Alfred Stanway

Alfred Stanway is a man I met when he left retirement in Australia to come to the United States to start a new theological seminary in Pittsburgh. He was 70 at the time.

As a young accountant in Australia, he had come to a deep faith in Christ, and had eventually gone to seminary and then to East Africa as a missionary in the 1930s. He stayed there for more than 30 years, eventually becoming a bishop in the Anglican Church. Of course, all those days were long past when I knew him, but his vitality and his example as a man of prayer moved me as none other has.

The Stanways' house was across the street from ours, and when I looked out the window of my study I could see the window of his study—a room that was also his place of prayer. No matter how early I arose in the morning, his light was already on. He told me that he had found he needed that time alone with God early in the morning before his wife arose. He showed me his two little books of prayer, in which he kept lists of names and situations about which he prayed faithfully.

Alf—as I came to know him—invited me to come and have tea with him every Friday afternoon. At the end of each visit he always prayed with me about the situations in my life that we had discussed. He used to say,

"Prayer, care, and you're there. A little faith in a great God is enough."

It was not just his faith that impressed me so much, but it was also his view of God. His God seemed to be bigger than mine, and therefore he trusted God more than most men I've known. His prayers were always brief, humble, and filled with simple trust. Prayer was as natural as breath to Alf—the normal, natural way he sought and found God's presence and God's help moment by moment. If you spent any time with Alf Stanway, you learned that prayer need not be formal, nor lengthy, nor filled with impressive words, or that a man doesn't need a theological education to build a strong, simple relationship with God.

Finally, prayer is a skill that matures us as we grow in our practice of it. And as we mature, we find that prayer becomes more authentic, more helpful, and more meaningful. Another of our former presidents taught us this truth through his own personal experiences.

Abraham Lincoln's Journey in Prayer

Even though Abraham Lincoln repeatedly called the entire American nation to days of prayer and fasting on behalf of our country, few historians regard him as a man of piety. But those who have carefully researched the life of Abraham Lincoln have been greatly impressed with the fact that Lincoln grew steadily in his relationship with God. He became a man who depended upon prayer. His prayers were informal, not read from a book. They were brief and to the point, full of humility and full of faith. Here was a man who prayed as though he knew God heard him. He was no sentimentalist—he was a man's man right down to his boots. After he had committed something to his Father in heaven, that was it. It didn't seem to trouble him anymore. He trusted God and got on with things.

As a young man, Lincoln was impressed by the faith and prayers of his mother. But as time went on, his great intellect got in the way. He believed in God, but had difficulty with the idea of a personal God. As he matured, however, he became more convinced, not just that God could be known, but that God's will could be discerned—and that became the chief concern in Lincoln's prayer life.

These words were found written out in his personal notes, and in his own hand: "It is more pleasing to God to see His people study Him and His will directly than to spend the first and chief of their efforts attaining comfort for themselves."

He viewed prayer as this: Seeking to put yourself into as close a relationship with God as possible in order to know and do His will.

Speaking once to a gathering of Presbyterian clergy, Lincoln said, "I was early brought to a living reflection that nothing in my power whatever ... would succeed without the direct assistance of the Almighty.... I have often wished that I was a more devout man than I am.... Nevertheless, amid the greatest difficulties of my administration, when I could not see any other resort, I would place my whole reliance in God."[2] His law partner, a man named Herndon, wrote that he never viewed Lincoln as a believer. But Herndon didn't know Lincoln in the crucial later years of his life. As the United States moved into civil war, the terrible weight of responsibility drove Lincoln back to God. Lincoln had never had any administrative experience when he became president, and he had to deal with the most terrible burdens imaginable. They drove him to his knees.

It wasn't that he had not been a believer and had not prayed before, but at last he became able to speak about prayer openly without embarrassment. It was the deepest experience of his life.

Elton Trueblood has written, "The evidence of Abraham Lincoln's own practice of personal prayer is so abundant that no thoughtful person can deny it. He prayed alone and he called the nation to prayer. He prayed for guidance and he prayed in gratitude. He prayed in defeat and he prayed in victory."[3] But prayer didn't come easily to him, as it doesn't come easily to most of us.

Often on a weeknight Lincoln would walk to the New York Avenue Presbyterian Church in Washington D.C., and sit unseen in the pastor's study with the door ajar while the evening prayer meeting was going on. "He told his pastor, Phineas Gurley, that he received important help from these simple, quiet gatherings. Chiefly because they were characterized more by prayer than by the making of speeches … Talking with God seemed to the mature Lincoln more important than talking about Him."[4] He worshiped regularly, and it is said that Lincoln always showed his personal respect for God in times of prayer by standing during the pastoral prayer as did a number of other men who attended that church.

Various contemporaries of Lincoln reported on the meaning that prayer came to have in the president's life. Lincoln's wife, for instance, said that on the day when he was first inaugurated president, he drew his family together and read to them a portion of the address that he was about to deliver. He then asked the family to join him in prayer as he prayed aloud for strength and guidance. Noah Brooks, the man who would have become his personal secretary had Lincoln lived longer, said that the president always observed the daily practice of prayer in spite of the demands of a busy schedule. Sometimes it would be only a few words. But he always took time for prayer.

His chief private secretary, who had perhaps as good an opportunity as any to know about Lincoln's private habits, said, "Mr. Lincoln was a praying man. I know that to be a fact and I have heard him request people to pray for him, which he would never have done had he not believed that prayer is answered."[5]

Lincoln was president for 49 months, and during that time he issued nine separate calls to the American people for public penitence, prayer, fasting, and thanksgiving. It was crucially important to him that people pray for the country. But Lincoln had to grow into this maturity. Horace Greeley, who was the editor of the *New York Tribune*, said about Lincoln: "Never before did one so constantly and visibly grow under the disciplines of incessant cares, anxieties, and trials. The Lincoln of 1862 was plainly a larger, broader, and better man than he had been in '61, while '63 and '64 worked his continued and unabated growth in mental and moral stature."[6]

Here's a statement from Lincoln to challenge you and me today. In calling a nation to prayer, he wrote of our American sin of self-sufficiency: "Intoxicated with unbroken successes, we have become too self-sufficient to feel the necessity of redeeming and preserving grace, too proud to pray to the God that made us."[7] Is this possibly true of us as men today?

It's Not Too Late to Learn

Isn't it true that most of us today still struggle with the same sins of self-sufficiency and pride? Our problems reveal to us the limits of our ability. But will we humble ourselves and pray? Like Lincoln, we may be embarrassed or indifferent about spiritual things, but we can grow into men of prayer. It is when we come to the end of our abilities to solve the matters before us that we finally have the possibility to learn how to depend upon God for help. We finally take more seriously our responsibility to discern God's will and follow it instead of our own.

You can, with God's help, begin to move from self-sufficiency to God-directedness now.

What Does It Mean to Be a Man Who Knows God?

Humility is the quality beyond all others that drives us honestly to God. It opens us up to help from beyond ourselves. The realization that we can't do it all ourselves drives us to look to someone beyond ourselves. If you carefully study the life of Christ, you will find that as the Son of God, He consistently made time for those people who came to Him after recognizing their own great need. Those who came to the Son of God in humility—which is the supreme and defining attribute of Jesus himself—were the ones in whose lives the Lord could truly do great things. Whether it was supplying practical needs at a wedding, or healing a distraught father's sick daughter, Jesus always exhibited a willingness to reach out and help those who knew that they could no longer help themselves. A humble heart is a heart in which our Almighty God has room to answer prayer.

God's Purpose or Your Own

God has His own purposes for you. He sees you and knows you. He is even more aware of your needs than you are.

Let me suggest that before you go any further in this book you take some time by yourself and simply, but thankfully, write out a prayer for yourself. When the Father looks at you, what would He like to see you become? Take time to consider this, and then write out a prayer for yourself asking God to change you and help you to experience and become the specific things you feel He'd like to see develop in you. Then, pray this prayer for yourself daily for at least a month. Let's see what happens.

For Thought and Discussion

1. When you make time to be alone in order to pray, what happens that makes it easier or more difficult for you to pray?

2. What do you think George Washington or Alf Stanway or Abraham Lincoln might say to you in the form of advice or encouragement as you seek to learn to pray?

3. Perhaps you'd like to write out here on this page, or in a private journal, your own personal prayer for yourself. Recognize that the Lord is with you. Ask Him what changes He wants to see in your life. Be honest and open. List them, and then turn them into a prayer asking God to do in your life those things that He wants to do.

1. The information on George Washington comes primarily from three documents:

   George Washington, As a Christian and Church Man; a monograph by Edward Slater Dunlap, published in 1932 by the Dean and Chaplain of Washington Cathedral, Mount St. Alban, Washington, D. C.

   How Washington Makes Us Think of the Church; a monograph by John S. Little, II, published in 1916 by The American Society of Church Literature.

   George Washington; a monograph by D. James Kennedy, published privately in Ft. Lauderdale, Florida, by Coral Ridge Presbyterian Church.

2. Elton Trueblood, *Abraham Lincoln: Theologian of American Anguish* (New York: Harper & Row Publishers, 1973.

3. Ibid., p. 74.

4. Ibid., p. 75.

5. Ibid., p. 89.

6. Ibid., p. 88.

7. Ibid., p. 088.

Getting to the Heart of Prayer 3

An amazing story came out of the Desert Storm war in the early '90s. Marine Major General Charles Krulak had been responsible to prepare supplies for a major frontal assault by the Allied forces against the Iraqi troops. Plans were made as the terrifying threat of chemical warfare loomed. It became apparent that there would be a great need for water, because decontamination procedures demand huge amounts of it. Krulak had enough water wells prepared to supply 100,000 gallons a day for the ground offensive—but then strategy changed. General Schwarzkopf announced a new plan that necessitated Krulak's moving his operations 74 miles to the northwest.

In that area, repeated attempts to find water were fruitless, as numerous drillings turned up only desert dust. The general consulted with oil companies, engineers, and Bedouins who knew the area well, all to no avail. Finally, they had exhausted all possible resources except the one that Krulak says he has turned to every morning since 1977, when he began a habit of praying with any staff members who wished to join him.

As General Krulak related his story to a group in Washington shortly after the war, he said he was on his knees praying for water one morning, only a few days before the ground attack was scheduled to begin. A colonel interrupted, asking Krulak to accompany him. As the two traveled down a road that had been built by the Marine Corps, they came upon something that sent chills up their spines.

About 50 yards off the road, they saw what seemed to be a pipe rising out of the ground. As they approached it, they saw a crossbar protruding from the pipe. The two men became incredulous. Here, in the middle of nowhere, was a brightly painted red pump and, at the base of the pipe, a green diesel generator with four new batteries still wrapped in plastic. Next to it was a tank above the ground with 1,000 gallons of diesel fuel stored in it. At that time, American forces didn't use diesel fuel. All the equipment was brand new and ready to go.

When Krulak pushed the start button, the new generator cranked up immediately and water started flowing. *The well produced within 10 gallons of the 100,000 gallons a day needed for the assault.*

General Krulak says he can't even recall how many times he had personally traveled up and down the road that ran by that pipe and not only he, but a division of men—2,000 troops—had also traveled it. No one had seen a water pipe until that morning. Krulak said, "There is no way anyone could have driven down that road and not seen that well and equipment painted in multiple colors." Perhaps there is a natural explanation. No matter. To Krulak, that well was an answer to prayer.

The former Archbishop for the Church of England, William Temple, is said to have commented, "When I pray, *coincidences* happen. When I don't pray, coincidences don't happen."

It has been the experience of men of God throughout the ages that "coincidences" like this do indeed grow out of prayer and are a part of the kind of life God wants us to experience. The God who created us wants to be involved in our day-to-day lives. An authentic and vital prayer life is at the heart of the relationship that God will allow us to have with Himself. When we look at the men and women of the Bible, we notice immediately how central prayer is to their everyday experience:

> *Noah* listened for God's voice and then listened for direction.
>
> *Moses* prayed for God's presence to go with Israel, for miracles, and for patience.
>
> *David* prayed for God's assistance, for a penitent spirit, and forgiveness.
>
> *Samuel* said that even though he was angry with Saul, it would be a sin if he didn't pray for him.
>
> *Solomon* prayed for wisdom.
>
> *Elijah* prayed for rain.
>
> *Hezekiah* prayed to be delivered from his enemies.
>
> *Jeremiah* prayed for more understanding when God's plan for the nation troubled him.

We notice the same thing when we read the New Testament and look at the life of the disciples, and we see that Jesus, the Son of God, prayed over and over again, by Himself and with others, in houses and in the wilderness. He not only prayed in all sorts of situations but He taught His disciples how to pray and said that men ought always to pray and never lose heart.

Jesus made striking, almost incredible, statements about prayer:

> *If you abide in me, and my words abide in you, ask for whatever you wish, and it will be done for you* (John 15:7, NRSV).

Therefore I say to you, all things for which you pray and ask, believe that you have received them, and they shall be granted you (Mark 11:24, NASB).

Again, I say unto you, that if two of you shall agree on earth as touching any thing that they shall ask, it shall be done for them of my Father which is in heaven (Matthew 18:19, KJV).

Paul said that even though we don't know how to pray, the Holy Spirit will help us. *Pray without ceasing,* he said (1 Thessalonians 5:17, NKJV). Many of Paul's prayers are recorded, and he urged others to pray for him.

The same is true of the apostles Peter, James, and John. There are so many examples of them praying or exhorting others to pray that we can hardly count them. Many of us are quick to ask the question, "How do I pray?" But before we try to answer that question in any detail, we first have to ask the question, "What exactly is prayer?" Unless we comprehend what prayer is, we may go through our entire lives with a total misunderstanding about how a man can pray.

What Exactly Is Prayer?

While it is crucial to come to God with our needs in an attitude of humility, prayer is much more than asking God's help. Prayer is actually keeping company with God. At its heart, prayer is the enjoyment of living out a friendship with God. Prayer is the way we communicate with our Creator.

A man asked me recently, "But how do I know God wants to hear from me? I haven't prayed in *years.* And how do I know He wants a friendship with me? If the Bible is true, I've broken most of His rules. I'm sorry I did and I want to change—but how do I know He'll take me back?"

Many men feel the same way. Who are *we* to go knocking on God's door? For lots of us, God the Father is distant, holy, and removed. Even the prophet Isaiah, when he had his famous vision of God in the temple 2,600 years ago, cried, "Woe is me!" when he saw God's holiness.

The remarkable thing is that God *does* care about you and me. He cared so much that He sent His Son into our world to introduce us to himself. Jesus taught us much through His life, teachings, and example. But through His death and resurrection, He actually covered our sins and opened the doorway to God. Now the door stands open and the Father invites us in.

Prayer is actually keeping company with God.

Yet some of us are afraid. There is too much we don't know about this great God. That's why God the Father and God the Son sent the Holy Spirit to take us by the hand, to lead us through the doorway and into His presence. The Holy Spirit is the one who puts our hand into God's. He teaches us how to have a friendship with God the Father. *That friendship is the heart of prayer.*

It's easy for a man to forget that praying is simply experiencing the presence of God. Many people talk more about the methods of prayer than the essence of prayer. They are quick to recommend various plans, orders, and schemes, such as beginning with worship, then moving to confession, then thanksgiving, and finally supplication. Others stress how important it is to fast during extended prayer times. Some put emphasis on maintaining a certain posture— standing with your hands raised, or kneeling, or getting down on your face. Others say you've got to have great faith when you pray, and some sound like it's also helpful to pray in a very loud voice. Others say someone should join you so that you have a person agreeing with you in prayer. While some use objects to help them pray, such as the rosary, others teach the value of speaking in tongues in prayer. Most of these formulas imply that prayer is getting God to do what you want Him to do. But asking is only one aspect of prayer.

Two Views of Prayer

I would like you to consider two views of the relationship you can experience in prayer.

Imagine that two close friends are spending time together—two men who have known each other for a very long time. They've shared in many experiences over the years and appreciate each other greatly, sharing in a strong manly love for each other. They do things together. They can talk or be silent. They laugh. There are times of seriousness and sadness … and plain fun.

There is no formula for a friendship like this. It simply involves being together. To be together is enough because it is a genuine joy. In a way, prayer is like that. Prayer is like spending time with your best friend.

Here's another picture:

Imagine spending time with a wise man who wants to train you to be successful in your vocation. You can learn much of what you need to know if you've come to the place where you *appreciate* and *listen* to this mentor. To move deeper in our relationship with the God who wants to teach and guide us, we have to get over our adolescent rebellions and become trainable.

Imagine this mentor as an older man who is rich in the wisdom of senior years. He is experienced in many ways simply by the fact that he has lived a long time. But he has also done well; he is honored and respected. He is in full possession of all his talents and faculties. He makes himself available to you because he sees you as a son and wants to have a mature, strong relationship with you. This is a tremendous opportunity. You have much to learn and he has much to offer, and so you both decide to make time to be with each other every day.

The benefit to you is that you experience the companionship of a wise, experienced man. You receive assistance and guidance, but you also learn to take responsibility. He has the happiness of seeing you grow and mature as he helps you, challenges you, and passes on his life's work to you.

These two images—the one of a longtime relationship between two old friends, and the other of a relationship between a young man and his mentor—can help you to see two important aspects of the relationship God desires to have with us, the kind of relationship a father and son can have with each other.

I can think of very few men who have strong relationships with older men or mentors—or even with their dads. Many have lost their fathers through death, some are in competition with their dads, and some are painfully alienated. But each man that I can think of *longs* for a closer relationship with his father. In our heart of hearts, whether we know it or not, *most of us want to be close to someone who can guide us.* I've been surprised over the years at the number of men who, sometime after their father's death, have experienced startlingly real dreams in which they encounter their fathers in a new and deeper kind of relationship. I believe that this is because we each long to be close to the man who gave us the gift of life.

Do you long for this kind of relationship? Scripture says that our Father in heaven longs and eagerly seeks for us to come to Him. Picture the father of the prodigal son in Jesus' parable, looking out the window as he waits and hopes for his son to come back. Have you ever considered the fact that you are being sought by the Father—that He desires to have a close, supportive relationship with you?

As we begin to enjoy this companionship with the Father, we realize that through it we can seek His assistance, look for guidance and wisdom, ask Him to direct us in contacts with other people, and ask Him to give us both responsibility and help in carrying it out.

No wonder Jesus said, "Men ought always to pray." We as God's sons are made for this close, loving relationship with our Father in heaven.

If we can see prayer as companionship, then it changes our whole understanding of prayer from asking for things to being with God in a conscious relationship. Let's look now at three facets to this relationship with God, which will help us move away from an immature picture of prayer to a mature daily experience.

GRATITUDE

When we talk about being grateful to God, it means simply enjoying the relationship with our Father in heaven because we realize how great and good He is.

Jesus exemplified this side of prayer when standing outside the tomb of Lazarus. He spontaneously proclaimed, *Father, I thank you that you have heard me* (John 11:41, NIV).

David shouted, *Glorify the Lord with me; let us exalt his name together* (Psalm 34:3, NIV).

One way in which you can deepen your relationship with God is to reflect with gratitude on His greatness and goodness. If you do this, you will find yourself desiring to honor Him with your life, not just your words.

I've found it helpful to reflect every morning upon the past 24 hours and to consider the different benefits and blessings that have come my way. They are always there, even during the most trying times. Before I know it, I'm thanking God for life and feeling greatly blessed.

HONESTY

The second facet of our prayer relationship with the Father is being honest about our own lives. Often this involves confession, repentance, and rededication. At our farmhouse, there is a drain pipe leading from the basement to an exit point out in the pasture. Sometimes the pipe's opening becomes clogged up with mud, dirt, or snow, and that causes the basement to flood when the washing machine is being used. If I don't keep that drainage pipe completely unplugged and clear, I have trouble on my hands.

Sometimes, my life begins to seem flooded with cares because I've *allowed* my life to become clogged with bad attitudes, wrong relationships, questionable habits, selfish or self-justifying thoughts, pride, self-pity, envy, or greed. Many men either feel that their job requires them to work long hours or they find very little satisfaction in their job, and they become saturated with self-pity. It's hard to have a relationship with someone when you're absorbed in your own problems.

Sometimes in our relationships with our wives or with our employers we may feel we're being unfairly attacked or criticized. As a result, we're prone to feel a great urge to justify ourselves. Our whole outlook is clouded by an obsession with our own anger and frustration. This makes prayer awfully difficult. So when we pray, we need to begin by examining ourselves, owning up to the anger or fear or jealousy that we are struggling with, and ask God to help us to be released from it. There is very little in life these days that encourages us toward careful self-examination, but it is essential to maturity and it's also a part of our prayer relationship with the Father. Sin—whether it be self-absorption or greed or distraction—can clog our relationship with God. We cannot overcome our shortcomings or sins without turning to God for help. At its heart, sin is against God, and we must deal with it in His presence.

For example, David fell away from God, committed adultery, and engineered a murder—and then tried to continue living as though everything was just fine. But it didn't work. Inwardly he was miserable because he was alienated from God. Finally he was confronted by a friend about his waywardness, and in coming to God one more time, he poured out his heart in repentance (see Psalm 51). Even though he had wronged many people, he began this psalm by admitting he had sinned against *God* and needed His forgiveness before all else.

The same is true of each of us men. We benefit greatly by *regularly reviewing our lives* and examining those sins for which we need to ask God's forgiveness and deliverance. Early in the morning is a good time to review the day past. It's a good time to consider your conversations, your manners, your attitude, whom you are putting first, whose agenda was most important to you in a recent meeting, what place God took in your life over the past day or two.... It helps periodically to meditate on certain passages of Scripture, particularly the Ten Commandments, or a portion of the Sermon on the Mount, which has a way of opening our eyes to see our sin.

This kind of confession helps us face the ways in which we turn away from God. We come back to Him in sincere apology. A prayer from our church's prayer book sums up the heart of confession effectively. Even if you are not into liturgical or written prayers, I think this confession nails it for most of us:

> … Merciful God,
> We confess that we have sinned against you
> in thought, word, and deed,
> by what we have done,
> by what we have left undone.
> We have not loved you with our whole heart.
> We have not loved our neighbor as ourselves.
> We are truly sorry and we humbly repent.
> For the sake of your Son, Jesus Christ,
> have mercy on us and forgive us,
> that we may delight in your will
> and walk in your ways,
> to the glory of your name. Amen.

What matters most, of course, is what's happening in your heart. John Bunyan, author of *Pilgrim's Progress*, once said, "In prayer, it's better to have the heart without words, than words without the heart." The Puritan Richard Sibbes said, "God can pick sense out of a confused prayer." What really matters in prayer is that we are in honest communion with God, simply giving ourselves to Him from the heart.

LISTENING

There is another important facet of our relationship with God—*listening*. Learning to listen to God is one of the hardest disciplines of prayer. It's one of the most crucial parts of any relationship, yet many men have lost the ability to hear God's voice.

How does God speak to us?

He will guide, teach, and correct through the Scriptures. Sometimes, too, we experience God's guidance through the wise counsel of another friend. Often He speaks to us through circumstances and experiences. But there are times as well when we need to sit quietly before God and let Him speak more intimately in the stillness of our souls. Our task is to learn to listen.

Sometimes His guidance comes through a sense of peace when, for instance, you are considering a difficult decision. You may have carefully thought through the situation, laid out the pros and cons, and sought the advice of others. But in the end, you need to come to God in silence and seek to be guided by His Spirit as He speaks to your spirit. Then, it is possible to experience the deepening sense of conviction that one way is right and the other wrong—and to act with confidence.

At other times, as you commit your way to Him, you will find that Scripture may leap out at you with special meaning. Occasionally, when you are quietly praying or being still before God, a name, an image, or an idea may come to mind. This can be another way that God breaks through into our consciousness and leads us in a new direction.

Slowly, as you learn to trust in God, you will understand what it is to sense His closeness and hear His voice.

There are, of course, other elements in a good relationship, and also other facets of prayer. There is intercession, for instance, in which we pray carefully for the needs of our family. We'll examine this more thoroughly a bit later.

> *As you learn to trust in God, You will understand what it is to sense His closeness and hear His voice.*

But for now, I want you to make a commitment to a time and place where you can meet with your heavenly Father. *We learn about prayer by praying.*

If we open all of our heart's contents to God—our hopes, dreams, needs, *and* failures—we will experience the gift of communion with Him. Then, as we seek His help, it will come. We can experience the wonder of personal forgiveness and restoration. We can grow in wisdom and character.

And it's in experiencing the touch of God that we become convinced of the love He has for us. This assurance and certainty comes through prayer.

For most of us, it just takes time.

For Thought and Discussion

1. Can you recall some specific incident in which God clearly and dramatically answered your prayer? What happened?

2. What do you think are some of the elements of a good, close, ongoing relationship with another person, and how do they relate to this notion of prayer being the heart of our relationship with God?

3. What are some of the sorts of attitudes you might develop that are likely to block your relationship with God?

4. Have you had situations in which you felt God did speak to you and gave you some sort of guidance or encouragement? What happened? What enabled you to hear from God in this way?

Barriers to Prayer 4

A man I know well—whom I'll call Tom—was facing a problem that affected his family.

The old family station wagon had reached its final stages of life and needed to be replaced—but there seemed to be absolutely no way Tom could pull together the resources necessary to purchase even a good used vehicle. Over and over he examined their finances, trying to figure out a way to afford *something*. He scoured the classified ads looking for a car that he could afford. But the more he worked at it, the more discouraged he became. Soon his concern about replacing the car became an even larger issue: It represented for him an inability as husband and father to provide adequately for his family.

As he became more discouraged, the old station wagon became a constant source of irritation, reminding him of his "failure" to do right for his family.

One night when the family was all together after supper, Tom decided to talk to his family about the situation. It was difficult to share with them the kinds of thoughts he was having—but he did. And as they sat together around the kitchen table talking and looking at the problem together, there was an unusual bond of closeness and understanding among them. Finally, someone suggested that as a family they ask God to help with this problem. Bowing their heads, they prayed about it together. Offhandedly, someone added to the prayer that it would certainly be great if God would give them a car that was especially safe—"like a Volvo or something."

It was a nice time. But as the family went to bed that night, Tom didn't feel any closer to a solution—though he did feel somewhat better for having talked and prayed about the matter with his family.

Two weeks after the family prayer time, Tom received a phone call from a local businessman. Only one or two other people knew about his family's need, but one of those people had apparently kept it in mind and mentioned the need to the man who was on the line. It just so happened that his company had a business vehicle that had depreciated to the point that they were getting ready to replace it. The businessman called to say that if my friend thought he could use it, he'd be glad to sell it to him for $1.00. It had some mileage on it, but had been maintained unusually well and it was in excellent condition. And by the way, it was a red Volvo.

To say that Tom was stunned is a great understatement. To say that he is a man who believes in prayer is also an understatement!

Sometimes people ask me about the problem of unanswered prayer. Frankly, I think a bigger problem is *unoffered* prayer. Why are we so slow in asking our Father in heaven to help us with our difficulties and challenges?

Paul reminds us that God is able to accomplish abundantly far more than all we can ask or imagine as we come to Him through Christ (Ephesians 3:20-21, NRSV). So why is it that I—even as a sincere believer—meet my needs and problems with worry, anger, or knee-jerk aggression? Why does it take me so long at times to make something a matter of discussion with my heavenly Father?

Let's take a look at four of the biggest barriers to prayer.

Barrier#1: Doubt

As men in a Western culture, we seem to have an inbred skepticism. Recently, a number of national surveys have pointed out the growing distrust that characterizes people in our culture. We don't trust politicians, the media, or religious leaders. Is it any wonder we have a difficult time trusting God?

C.S. Lewis said, "The trouble with me is lack of faith…. The irrational dead weight of my old skeptical habits and the spirit of this age and the cares of the day steal away all my lively feeling of the truth, and often when I pray I wonder if I am not posting to a nonexistent address. Mind you, I don't think so—the whole of my reasonable mind is convinced: but I often *feel* so."

I was raised in a part of North Carolina that is "dry," which means that alcoholic beverages may not legally be sold in our area. It was said that a tavern was being built in a town that *had* been dry. But a group of Christians in a church opposed this and began an all-night prayer meeting asking God to intervene. When lightning struck the bar and it burned to the ground, the owner subsequently brought a lawsuit against the church, claiming those praying had been responsible! The Christians hired a lawyer, claiming they were not responsible, and the judge said, "No matter how this case comes out, one thing is clear. The tavern owner believes in prayer and the Christians do not."

There is an odd, even humorous, element to this story—but how often do we pray without believing?

Making a good marriage and having a godly influence upon our kids is such a huge challenge today, and we're tempted to doubt that God can or will work in the lives of our children or our wife.

◆ Our world is so saturated with sex, and the promiscuity of young people is so widely accepted, that it seems too much for us to believe our children can actually maintain their sexual purity until marriage.

◆ In many public schools there is such an "anti-Christian" bias that we sometimes wonder if our kids can salvage any kind of faith at all in the face of cynicism and even ridicule.

◆ When your wife has been smoking for 20 years and shows no inclination to stop—or she's chronically ill, or depressed—it's hard to believe that your prayers can have any impact.

◆ When your little boy is an outcast, or your son is booted out of college, or your daughter can't hold a job, it's hard to believe God can turn situations and people around.

Problems are real. Challenges are overwhelming. And there is something in us that automatically doubts God and holds us back from trusting Him.

Satan is recorded speaking only three times in all of Scripture. First, in the garden of Eden when he causes Adam and Eve to doubt the truth of God's Word ... to doubt God. Second, he spoke to God trying to make God doubt His servant Job. And Satan spoke to Jesus in the wilderness, seeking to make Jesus doubt himself as the Son of God. Whatever the source of our doubts, when it becomes difficult for us to believe in God, our tendency is always to turn away from Him. But where or to whom are we going to turn? There is nothing wrong in asking the help and advice of others in dealing with family challenges—but it's a mistake not to take our needs to God first.

Even when our faith is weak, prayers for our family can begin by asking God to help us to have *more* faith. A man in the New Testament came to Jesus and said, *I do believe; help me overcome my unbelief* (Mark 9:24, NIV). It's as though we have two distinct appetites—one is for doubt, and one is for faith. The truth is, the appetite we feed is the one that will grow. By choosing not to doubt, you can choose to have your faith grow.

James wrote,

> *If any of you is lacking in wisdom, ask God, who gives to all generously and ungrudgingly, and it will be given you. But ask in faith, never doubting, for the one who doubts is like a wave of the sea, driven and tossed by the wind; for the doubter, being double-minded and unstable in every way, must not expect to receive anything from the Lord* (1:5-8, NRSV).

The unknown apostle who wrote to the Hebrews put it very plainly when he said,

> *Without faith it is impossible to please God, for whoever would approach him must believe that he exists, and that he rewards those who seek him.* (11:6)

Jesus himself made the following declaration:

> *Have faith in God. Truly I tell you, if you say to this mountain, 'Be taken up and thrown into the sea,' and if you do not doubt in your heart, but believe that what you say will come to pass, it will be done for you. So I tell you, whatever you ask for in prayer, believe that you have received it, and it will be yours* (Mark 11:22-24, NRSV).

But how do we get this sort of faith? Let me suggest two simple steps.

The Bible describes faith as a gift of God. It's not something that we can conjure up. So the first way to get faith is simply to ask God to increase it. Ask Him regularly to help you become a man of greater faith.

Second, whatever faith you have needs to be fed so it will grow. The way we feed our faith is by focusing on Christ and meditating on the strong, true, faithful character of God. Scripture shows us that He is not only all-wise and just, but He is kind, good, loving, observant of our needs, and responsive. He's also all-powerful—nothing is impossible for Him. It nourishes and strengthens the soul to remember that God's character is the source of our faith when we pray. We don't focus on what little faith we have, but we focus on the mighty God we serve. That is, we don't get more faith by *trying* to have more faith; rather, our faith grows as God becomes greater in our souls.

As adults, many of us have lost faith and need to recapture it. So often we have thoughts such as, "God is not interested," or, "This is not important to God," or, "Prayer is not real, anyway." The answer is not to feed these doubts by focusing on them, but instead to feed our faith by reminding ourselves about the character of God as He has presented himself to us in Scripture— particularly as Jesus Christ presents God to us as a Father who listens, cares, and answers when we call.

As a young man, I had many battles with doubt. I knew I needed to do something to feed and strengthen my faith. So when my first child was born, I wrote out a little list of simple prayers on her behalf, which I prayed several times each week. (I will say more about this later on in this book.) This became a habit, and has been consistent with all of my children. I have many lists of simple prayer requests that I have made on behalf of each child over and over again through the years. As time has gone by and I have seen these prayers answered, I've jotted down the many ways God has worked. I can tell you, there is nothing that will banish doubt and strengthen faith like seeing your prayers answered!

How often do we fail to note how God has answered our prayers? Then we miss the faith-strengthening that comes when we see how God has met our needs and helped us with our concerns. Why not start your own prayer notebook—and begin to see how faithful God really is!

Barrier#2: Busyness

The second major barrier that keeps us from becoming men of prayer is the universal problem of *time*.

Prayer does take time. It can't be just crowded in. It has to be a *priority*. Sometimes we tell ourselves that our family needs us to be busy and a successful breadwinner. We justify our lack of prayer by saying that we're just being responsible for the family and that we don't have time to pray. The quick "prayer-on-the-run" is okay—as an exception. But *not* as the rule. In one way, prayer is like sex in marriage: Over the long run, you won't be satisfied unless you make the time to do it right. Jesus made a time and a place for prayer regularly. The reason for this is that prayer demands a focus and full devotion of one's self.

It does sometimes take us a little while to slow down and actually focus on the God to whom we are praying. In a sense, this is like conversation with another person. My wife used to say to me in the early days of our marriage,

"Look at me when we're talking. Look at me and listen, so I know you're thinking about what I'm saying." The same thing is true with God. We cannot expect our ability to know Him to grow if we are superficial and casual about prayer. I had some ability in tennis once, but I never achieved my potential because I was never willing to make it a priority. I didn't particularly care, but this frustrated other people who believed in me and wanted me to excel. How frustrating it must be to God when we don't make being with Him a priority.

We have to decide once and for all, "I'm going to be a man of prayer, and I'm going to make the commitment of time." It's not enough just to ask God to help you become a man of prayer, you've got to *do it*.

Men, do you care enough about your families to set aside a regular time and place to pray for them? I've learned over the years that we really do have time to do whatever is most important to us. If something is important, we can make the time for it by crowding out other things. We can tell ourselves we don't have time to pray, but the fact is we do. It's a question of deciding what's important.

Take an honest hard look at how you spend your time and you'll see clearly what is valuable to you.

The same is true if you want to pray together as a family. You have to decide to do it and then take the initiative. Whether you pray after dinner or in the morning or kneeling at your child's bed, it takes commitment—whether you *feel* like it or not.

Before we were married, my wife and I decided that as a married couple we would pray together every night at bedtime. There have been times, over these many years, when we certainly haven't felt like it, but when we have pushed through the "I don't feel like it" attitude and taken the time, the rewards have come.

Very few activities will strengthen both your marriage and your relationship to God as much as praying together as a couple. For my wife and me, the commitment to pray together every night has become a crucial habit. Every night after we are in bed, with the light off, I offer a very simple prayer, often lasting no more than 60 seconds. I thank God for the blessings of the day; I ask His care for our children; I bring before Him other situations that are on our minds. This simple discipline has made all the difference in the world in our relationship with each other, as it has ensured that at least once a day the two of us together are turning our full attention to God. This strengthens our relationship with God—and it has forced us on many occasions to deal with problems between us, things that would make it impossible for us to pray until we first dealt with our attitudes toward each other.

This leads to the third barrier preventing us from becoming men of prayer.

Barrier#3: Wrong Relationships

Many times the problem is not a lack of discipline or a lack of faith. Often the barrier is in our relationship with God, or with a member of our family. When we have sinned or have strained relationships, we cannot grow as men of prayer. Jesus said, *And when you stand praying, if you hold anything against anyone, forgive him, so that your Father in heaven may forgive you your sins* (Mark 11:25, NIV). Similarly, in another place He said, *Therefore if you are offering your gift at the altar and there remember that your brother has something against you, leave your gift there in front of the altar. First go and be reconciled to your brother, then come and offer your gift* (Matthew 5:23-24, NIV).

Chapter 4: Barriers to Prayer

When we have wronged someone or sinned against God, and we are unwilling to reconcile, it is an indication of hidden pride—and how can we come to God with this deeper sin buried in our souls?

Over the years I've observed that wrong relationships between people are perhaps the *greatest* roadblock to the work of God going forward. Similarly, if there's something between us and God, we are prevented from going forward in prayer. The prophet Isaiah pointed out to the people of his day, *Your iniquities have been barriers between you and your God, and your sins have hidden His face from you so that He does not hear* (Isaiah 59:2, NRSV). If there is any possibility that a wrong relationship or a wrong action will keep God from hearing your prayers, it's not worth it to persist in those activities and attitudes—there's just too much at stake. The psalmist said, *If I had cherished iniquity in my heart, the Lord would not have listened* (Psalm 66:18, NRSV). He wrote about the relief that he experienced when at last he sought and found God's forgiveness: *Truly God has listened; He has given heed to the words of my prayer. Blessed be God because He has not rejected my prayer or removed His steadfast love from me* (Psalm 66:19-20, NRSV).

Maybe the reason your prayer life is going nowhere is that there are things in your life that are displeasing to God—attitudes or actions that you've been rationalizing and accepting. Sure, you can still pray—but your prayer life will produce little. This is why it can be so important to pray with another person. Jesus emphasized this, saying, *If two of you on earth agree about anything you ask for, it will be done for you* (Matthew 18:19-20, NIV). There's something about bowing to pray with another person that sensitizes your conscience. It puts you on red alert to your own ego when you're praying with another man—or a small group of men—who know you well.

Once when I was praying with a group of men, another man interrupted right in the middle of my prayer. He said he simply could not agree with me in that particular prayer because he knew me and believed my attitude was wrong. This sparked a discussion that was difficult but tremendously helpful for me in dealing with some things in my own life that I'd been ignoring. Praying with our wives, or praying with another man, pushes us to confront ourselves as we really are—to confess our sins, to understand ourselves better, to ask forgiveness, and to become forgivers. Praying with another person forces us to be reconciled, and strengthens our relationship with each other. I believe this is what Peter had in mind when he wrote the following words to husbands: *Husbands … show consideration for your wives in your life together, paying honor to the woman as the weaker sex, since they too are also heirs of the gracious gift of life—so that nothing may hinder your prayers* (1 Peter 3:7, NRSV). If a man's relationship with his wife is not right, his prayer life is going to be hindered, and their prayer life together will be impossible.

In the Church of the first century, the followers of Christ took this principle quite seriously. When they met for worship on the first day of the week, they always shared in Holy Communion together. But after the time of teaching from the Scripture, and before they joined together in communion, it became their custom to take a break when they would "exchange the peace" with one another. It was during this time that the people were instructed to get things straight with other members of the Christian family. It was understood that you would never go to communion if your relationship with someone else in the family of Christ was not healthy and whole. Over the centuries since then, when Christians have practiced this discipline of keeping relationships right, day by day, it has strengthened the Church. It will strengthen your family, too, if you learn to go to whichever member of the family you may be having a difficult time with and do all you possibly can to come to a better understanding and make it right immediately.

Even during that time in a teenager's life—between 13 and 17—when it's often difficult to have a peaceful relationship with your child, a father needs to maintain a close relationship with his son or daughter. If he ever senses that something has come between them, the wise father will take the initiative to spend some time with that child, sooner rather than later. Many times I've had to go to my son or daughter and apologize, asking forgiveness for a hasty word or a thoughtless action. Sometimes I make mistakes without realizing it, and come to grips with the problem when my wife points out the error, or when in the silence of my prayer time, I finally get quiet enough to allow the Holy Spirit to point out my sins.

It's always the right time to go and make a problem right. Some of the hardest but most precious times I've had with Susan and my children have been when we've prayed together after making apologies. Your family relationships will go much deeper as a result of times like that.

Whenever there is something wrong in your relationship with a member of your family that is not dealt with quickly, it has the possibility of festering and driving a wedge between you. Doing all that can be done, with God's help, to keep relationships right with one another in the family is a central responsibility of the man who wants to be a spiritual leader in his home.

Barrier #4: Wrong Actions

Like wrong relationships, tolerating sin in other areas of our lives keeps us from growing in the relationship God wants to have with us. Expecting God to answer our prayers in spite of such actions is folly.

The tribes of Israel were defeated in a costly battle at a place called Ai. Even though they had been doing very well up to that point in their conquest of the Promised Land, and though they had asked for God's help as they were going into battle, they suffered a terrible loss. The reason for the loss eventually became clear after Joshua, their leader, tore his clothes and fell on his face before God begging for an answer. He was given the following one: *Israel has sinned; They have transgressed my covenant.... They have taken some of the devoted things; They have stolen, they have acted deceitfully, and they have put them among their own belongings* (Joshua 7:11, NRSV). Their sins had brought defeat and blocked their prayers.

Hypocrisy is one of the things we dislike the most in others, and we're quick to observe it, aren't we? But sometimes we're slow to see it in ourselves. We can tolerate a shading of the truth or a lack of complete honesty in paying our taxes and somehow let them go. But men, when we realize that we're guilty of cheating or lying or stealing, *if we are wise* we will turn away from it immediately—or it will crush our relationship with God.

Years ago I had a friend I'll call Mark who was just beginning to grow in his faith, and who was experiencing terrible marriage problems at the same time. He had developed a relationship with a woman in his office who seemed to care for and understand him in a way that his wife could not. Eventually, Mark moved in with the other woman. Another Christian man who knew him and cared about him lovingly confronted Mark regarding his wrong action. Mark defended his moving in with the other woman: "But I've never been loved like this before. I just can't tell you how good it is. If it feels so good, how could it possibly be wrong?" The friend assured him that it *was* wrong, and that it would only make matters worse in his relationships with his family and with God.

Because deep in his heart Mark wanted to be right with God, he did repent and move out. Now Mark is a strong leader in church renewal on the West Coast. He was wise to listen to his friend. Many men have seen their marriages, their families, and their careers utterly shipwrecked because they could not bring themselves to face up to and acknowledge the sin in their lives. Sooner or later, the man who steals on the job will have to pay a huge price. The man who abuses his family will be brought down. The adulterer will fall. It just doesn't make sense to tolerate wrong actions in our lives.

A Plan

I have found it to be particularly helpful to commit myself, in advance, to a particular plan for dealing with each of these four barriers.

The barrier of doubt will be gradually overcome if you establish the habit of daily Bible reading, weekly worship, and regular prayer. Participation in a small men's fellowship group and reading good Christian biographies helps, as well.

The barrier of busyness will be overcome if you set aside a daily time purely for prayer. Set a time. Pick the place. And *be there*. Do this, and over time a habit will begin to form.

Our family always has prayer together at breakfast. I may be away at an early meeting, or the family may be running late, but we made a commitment, before the children were born, to pray at the end of breakfast—and whomever is at home participates. It's our habit.

At 6:30 a.m., I habitually take my wife a cup of coffee, sit beside the bed with her for five or 10 minutes, and pray with her. It's what we do because we have established the habit.

When my friend Charlie Powell and I meet together, we have an unspoken commitment always to pray together for each other at the end of the meeting. It's become our pattern. As a church staff, we have set the time of 8:30-9:00 a.m. every day to meet together for prayer. It's become our habit.

The barrier of wrong relationships can be done away with if you decide *now*, once and for all, that whenever you become aware of something in your life that is wrong, you're going to own up to it, admit it to God and to others (if necessary), and ask God's forgiveness.

The barrier of sin is probably the most subtle. For me, it has been helpful to have another man in whom I can confide when I become aware that something is wrong in my life. If I'm harboring anger or irritation toward someone, or if I am aware of lust toward a woman, I can tell my friend. I ask him to advise me and to pray for me as far as knowing how to deal with it. He can hold me accountable to commitments I make. This has proved to be a wise and healthy habit.

In each of these four areas, we can commit ourselves to a particular plan and then ask God to help us stick to it. Habit alone cannot guarantee effectiveness or authenticity in one's prayer life. But I can promise you that if you establish these disciplines of prayer, confession, and spiritual fellowship, you will see yourself grow as a man of prayer.

For Thought and Discussion

1. Is doubt a major problem for you in the area of prayer, or does it only creep up on you periodically? Have you noticed any sources of, or reasons for, the periodic doubt that you experience?

2. When and where will you make prayer your first priority? What changes might you have to make in your schedule in order for this to happen?

3. Can you remember a time when a wrong relationship or a wrong action came between you and God? Did you deal with it? How?

4. Is there a barrier to effective prayer in your life right now that you need to deal with? How will you deal with it?

Turning Points in a Man's Prayer Life 5

We hope that as we grow older we'll become wiser as we learn from experiences. We *hope*.

The other day a friend of mine and I returned to his car only to find that he had locked his keys inside. While I was quietly feeling despair, Dick, who is in his 80's, said, "Well, it doesn't matter. I always carry an extra set of keys in my pocket." A long time before, he had learned his lesson.

Once I had the privilege of sitting on a crusade platform behind Billy Graham while he was addressing a huge outdoor gathering. I noticed that the pages of his notes were individually wrapped with plastic. He had evidently learned years ago to be prepared in case it started to rain before he finished his talk.

As men, we want to learn from our mistakes and put that wisdom to work—whether it's in the area of financial planning, or fishing, or caring for the car or the house. Unfortunately, I've had to learn a number of things the hard way. The first car my wife and I owned had a leaky transmission. We had to pay a great price because I—who didn't know much about cars—never kept track of the fluid level. Because of that expensive lesson, I learned to be alert for even the smallest slippage in that or *any* transmission.

Learning from life does pay off. I can tell you that, too.

Not long ago, I had another experience with my car that made me glad I've wised up about automobiles.

Recently I felt that there was something not quite right with the brakes but, non-mechanic that I am, I couldn't tell what it was. I took the car to a garage and the mechanic checked it out but said there was no problem. Still, I was uneasy. So I took it to another garage, and again was told the brakes were just fine. My son, who is in college, wanted to borrow this car to drive several hours to the mountains of West Virginia on a ski trip—but my uneasiness persisted.

In the end, even though two mechanics had told me there was nothing to worry about, I arranged for my son to use another car.

On the very same day that he would have been driving my Ford along snowy roads in the mountains, the brakes seized up and overheated. I spent the rest of the day in a garage having new brakes installed. If I had allowed my son to use the car, he could have broken down in the middle of nowhere, or skidded off a snowy mountain road when the brakes locked.

How glad I was that day, even for the hard lessons I'd learned along the way.

Throughout your life, you can learn a few basic truths through your own experience that will become the foundation of your relationship with God—*if* you set out on the adventure that prayer can be.

Earlier, we talked about learning to be open to God in our weaknesses and in our needs. Also we spoke about listening in stillness, and setting aside a special time and place for prayer. If we make even these first steps, we'll make several discoveries that will become major turning points in learning to pray for those we love.

Turning Point #1: Prayer Is Real

There was a time in my life when I assumed that prayer was real—but then I began to doubt. Perhaps prayer was just a placebo to make a person feel better.

As mentioned in the previous chapter, one of the favorite strategies of the enemy of our souls is to make us doubt God—to doubt His goodness, His care, His existence, or His interest in our need. How can you possibly pray when you think prayer is not real or is useless?

It's not that I was an unbeliever. I was a Bible-reading, praying Christian. I saw that men of God in the Bible always prayed—but, honestly, I was skeptical.

For me, the major turning point was the lesson my wife taught me about praying specifically. Susan loves the words of the apostle: *You have not because you ask not* (James 4:2, NKJV). Over and over again she has reminded me of this simple principle: *Ask.* She reminds me to be specific in my prayers. And I've found that *praying specifically* has taught me that *prayer is real.*

When Susan and I were first engaged to be married, we made a list of several prayer requests. We agreed to offer these prayers to God on a regular basis during our engagement. After the wedding, we completely forgot about our list—and we stumbled upon it only recently while cleaning out an old filing cabinet. The pages had yellowed over 25 years—but we were overwhelmed to see that one of our prayers during the engagement was that God would give us twins. Neither of us remembered praying for this, but God had indeed given us twins *10 years* after we were married!

As I mentioned earlier, when we were looking for a home several years ago, we agreed to pray specifically for the things we felt we needed and came up with a long list. We prayed for very practical matters such as price and location, but also for some aesthetic concerns as well. In the end, every request we made of God regarding this house was answered … except one. We wanted to have the house by a particular date. (We learned that our Father in heaven *is* very concerned about the details of our life but that we can't impose our schedule on Him!)

Friends of ours once told us of an experience they'd had in seeing prayer answered rather dramatically for one of their sons. Although they had a lot of confidence in his judgment, they were worried one evening because he had begun to go out with a girl whose morals were questionable. It was one of those situations in which parents realize they have to hold back, say little, but pray *much*!

When their son left in the car to pick up this girl one Saturday, our friends stopped for a few minutes to pray for him. They felt urged to pray that he would be kept from making a mistake in his relationship with this girl that he would later regret.

Later that evening, they had a telephone call. A policeman was on the line and wanted to talk to them about their son! It seems that he and his date had pulled off the road into a dark, romantic area and were alone necking in the car. The patrolman happened to see them, and he pulled over to tell them they were not in a safe area, that they had to move, and that he was going to report to the boy's parents that he had found them there. Needless to say, it shook these two kids up tremendously.

To this day, our friends look back to that experience as a significant moment in their son's life—he realized how careful he had to be about becoming too involved physically with young women. And it was a significant moment when they learned that prayer is real.

Remember, there is nothing about which we cannot pray. Wise men pray specifically for concerns in their own lives and in the lives of their wives and children. We pray knowing that our Father hears and cares. *Which of you, if his son asks for bread, will give him a stone? Or if he asks for a fish, will give him a snake? If you, then, though you are evil, know how to give good gifts to your children, how much more will your Father in heaven give good gifts to those who ask Him!* (Matthew 7:9-11, NIV).

Some worry that making specific requests of God might be presumptuous. It's true that God is in no way obligated to grant our every request. In His wisdom, He may answer *yes, no,* or *wait—the time is not right for this.* He wants us to ask because He loves us as a Father. This leads us to another major turning point.

Turning Point #2: Discovering God as Your Father

For much of my life, I thought of God as a distant blur. When I came to really know Him as my Father in heaven, it was a major turning point.

My own dad was a kind, dependable gentleman. He was approachable and generous, a man of utter integrity. He wouldn't put up with deceitfulness in any form. I remember him being consistently gracious. He certainly was not perfect. He had his own insensitivity and blind areas, as all men do, but he was a good man, and he loved me. The fact that he *was* a good man helped me later come to understand the goodness of God. A time came when I began to see the Father in heaven as caring for me—as my own father had done—but much more so.

Consider what Jesus said about God:

> *Your heavenly Father is perfect* (Matthew 5:48, RSV, italics mine).
> That means He is perfect goodness.

> *Your Father sees in secret* (Matthew 6:4, RSV).
> That means He knows my secret needs.

> *Your Father knows what you need…. Your heavenly Father knows that you need them all* (Matthew 6:8, 32, RSV).

> *Look at the birds they neither sow nor reap nor gather … and yet your heavenly Father feeds them. Are you not of more value than they?* (Matthew 6:26, RSV).

Jesus stressed the point that if we want to do good things for our children, how much more does our heavenly Father want to do good things for us?

> *What do you think? If a shepherd has a hundred sheep, and one of them has gone astray, does he not leave the ninety-nine on the mountains and go in search of the one that went astray? And if he finds it, truly I tell you, he rejoices over it more than the ninety-nine that never went astray. So it is not the will of your Father in heaven that one of these little ones should be lost* (Matthew 18:12-14, NRSV).

> *If two of you on earth agree about anything … it will be done for you by my Father in heaven. For when two or three are gathered in my name I am there among them* (Matthew 18:19, NRSV).

It is instructive to study what Jesus taught about God as our Father in the gospels. In John's gospel alone, God is referred to as Father more than 100 times, and the message of Jesus that comes to us through John seems to be: *The Father himself loves you* (John 16:27, NRSV).

If you had a father who was not good or did not care about you, or if you had a father who was not present or who was not giving, it would be difficult to see God as a loving heavenly Father. But God wants to heal these hurtful, imperfect images of fatherhood. If accepting God's fatherhood is difficult for you, ask Him to help you come to see Him in this way more and more.

A man I'll call Ken had a hard time accepting the fatherhood of God. One night he had a strange and vivid dream.

Ken's father had been dead for 15 years, but he dreamed that his dad came to him right there in the bedroom. He felt a powerful presence; it seemed to be much more than a dream. Ken's father stood at his bedside and smiled, then and held out his arms. Ken reached out to accept his father's embrace, and was enveloped in an overwhelming sense of love, peace, and well-being that he'd never experienced before. He felt engulfed in his father's love, overwhelmed at his closeness.

In the days that followed, Ken pondered the dream. It seemed like a special gift and held great significance. Mainly, as a result of the dream, Ken came to a much deeper understanding of the love his heavenly Father had for him. He knew that as great as his earthly father's love had been for him, the love of God the Father was greater still.

Grasping God's relationship to us as Father can radically impact the way we come to Him when we pray. I usually begin my prayers with the words, "Dear Father ..." For me personally, it is most helpful to see God in this way as I present my family's needs.

Turning Point #3: Keep On Asking

Jesus commanded those who followed Him to *ask*, to *seek*, and to *knock*. A more accurate way of translating what He said would be like this: *Ask and keep on asking, seek and keep on seeking, knock and keep on knocking.*

For reasons best understood by God, He often chooses to take His time in answering our prayers. Jesus illustrated this in a fairly unusual story, which is recorded in Luke 11.

Suppose one of you has a friend, and he goes to him at midnight and says, Friend, lend me three loaves of bread, because a friend of mine on a journey has come to me, and I have nothing to set before him. Then the one inside answers, Don't bother me. The door is already locked, and my children are with me in bed. I can't get up and give you anything. I tell you, though he will not get up and give him the bread because he is his friend, yet because of the man's boldness he will get up and give him as much as he needs. So I say to you: Ask and it will be given to you; seek and you will find; knock and the door will be opened to you. For everyone who asks receives; he who seeks finds; and to him who knocks, the door will be opened (v. 5-10, NIV).

I've alluded to the fact that, over the years, I've found it helpful to jot down my prayer requests in a notebook. I now have many notebooks filled with lists of prayers that I've prayed over and over again, particularly for other people. Skimming through these, I find a place where I've prayed for friends about their lonely child. Here's a prayer for a happier job for my godson. Here's a prayer for a friend to be more appreciated and to develop a greater sense of purpose. Here is a prayer for one of my children to find a sport that he can love and excel in.

These notebooks have become a record of the precious acts of God in response to the needs of my family and friends. (I'll say more about this in chapter 9.)

Why don't you consider beginning your own prayer notebook, recording the requests you bring to God on behalf of your family? Pray for your children—and your children's children. Who knows how generations of your family yet to come may be affected by your prayers?

Not long ago I was riding in a taxi. My driver, whose name was Gordon Murray, was not only dependable and courteous (as was printed on his business card), but I found him to be an ardent follower of Christ. He admitted that it had not always been so, but that over the years he'd come to realize that the two most important things in his life were his family and his faith.

"It sounds to me as though someone was praying for you," I offered.

He laughed. "You're right. I had a praying grandmother. Everybody ought to have one!"

He's right. Everybody ought to have someone who is praying for them persistently. But why do we almost exclusively hear about praying grandmothers? Wouldn't it be great for your grandkids to hear they had a praying grand*father*—a man who persisted in prayer for his family?

Men, *persistence* is a trait many of us lack. Bringing our prayer requests to God repeatedly is not a matter of asking God—and then reminding Him over and over again in case He's forgotten. No, when we persist in prayer it helps us to grow in our awareness that God *is* the Sovereign Ruler of all things, and it reminds us of our dependence upon Him. Yes, it's wonderful when you pray for something only once and you experience God's answer. But growth and maturity come when you learn how to pray repeatedly, until you have the satisfaction of seeing clearly how God has answered.

Perseverance in prayer is no guarantee that what you ask will come about in your lifetime. Nonetheless, we are to be obedient to Christ, who said to ask and keep on asking.

Turning Point #4: Learning to Pray in Jesus' Name

Jesus said, *I will do whatever you ask in my name, so that the Father may be glorified in the Son* (John 14:13-14, NRSV). Does this mean that Jesus offered us a blank check and that He will do whatever we want Him to do? Some Christians may say *yes*, but I disagree.

In part, I believe Jesus is warning us to pay attention to our prayers. Do we have the attitude of Christ when we pray?

Think of your prayer as a letter written to God. Would Jesus sign His name to your letter? If you can't imagine Jesus joining you in that request, then you're probably not able to pray that prayer in His name. Remember, He also told His disciples, *If you remain in me and my words remain in you, ask whatever you wish, and it will be given you* (John 15:7, NIV). This means that we need to measure the content of our prayers against the life and teachings of Christ.

Yes, the Bible offers promises, like this one: *This is the confidence we have in approaching God: that if we ask anything according to His will, He hears us. And if we know that He hears us—whatever we ask—we know that we have what we asked of Him* (1 John 5:14-15, NIV). Sometimes we're better off to preface our prayers by saying, *I don't know, Lord, if this is pleasing to you. But here it is ...*

A turning point in a man's prayer life comes when he learns not to presume upon God, or to demand from Him, or to bargain with Him. Instead, learn to ask: Would Jesus agree with my prayer? Would He agree with my attitude in making this request of God? Could I imagine Jesus saying something like this Himself? Could I imagine Jesus taking this step I'm prayerfully considering? Would the Lord agree with this decision I'm making?

If we don't have the assurance that what we're asking or seeking is something that would be pleasing to Christ, then it's better to slow down and give the matter further consideration.

Turning Point #5:
It's Okay If You Don't Know How to Pray

Situations are going to arise in which we simply don't know the "right way" to pray. Times will come when we can't seem to pray at all.

Perhaps you and your wife are having some big difficulties. Maybe a child is in trouble, and you are torn and don't know which direction to turn. Perhaps you and your family are in disagreement about something and you don't know who's right. You may wonder: "Do I pray for deliverance from my problems or do I pray for the strength to endure them? Do I pray for this thing I think I must have or do I pray for a changed heart?"

The apostle Paul felt the same confusion, I believe, when he wrote: *We do not know what we ought to pray for, but the Spirit Himself intercedes for us with groans that words cannot express. And He who searches our hearts knows the mind of the Spirit, because the Spirit intercedes for the saints in accordance with God's will* (Romans 8:26-27, NIV). There have been many times when

I've found myself ignorant, weak, uncertain, and inarticulate. Most men I know are aware of life's frailty and its ambiguities. Often, we simply won't know what's right. Paul says the Holy Spirit in us will help us pray, and He will actually intercede for us through our own inarticulate groans and through the thoughts we cannot express in words (or as one translator has rendered it: *with sighs too deep for words* (Romans 8:26, NRSV).

When we long to see good come of a situation but do not even know what to ask, God's Spirit joins us in our pain, confusion, difficulty, or uncertainty. And He prays to the Father on our behalf.

> *Envisioning God as our loving heavenly Father helps us to believe that He is hearing and responding to our prayer.*

When one of our daughters was a little girl, she would sometimes be overcome with sadness, fear, frustration, or uncertainty. This would result in anger, fighting, or lashing out at me. Rather than being put off or angry, I knew it was sadness and hurt inside that was causing her behavior. On some occasions, she would be so frustrated that she would finally collapse in my arms in tears. All I could do was cry with her. I could see ahead that all would be well in the end, but she couldn't. Even so, my heart would break and I'd try to comfort her. During those moments, I'd pray for her silently, holding her before the Father in heaven, asking Him to comfort and touch her in the depths of her spirit where I could not go. The Holy Spirit exercises this kind of ministry in our lives.

Coming to this realization years ago helped me to understand that even when I sit desolate and wordless before God, He is caring for my family and me.

Prayer is, indeed, real. Envisioning God as our loving heavenly Father helps us to believe that He is hearing and responding to our prayer. When we don't see a response to our prayers, we are to simply keep on asking until our needs change, or the situation changes, or until our heart changes. Always we must ask ourselves, "Is this a prayer that I can pray in Jesus' name?"

Even when we can't find the words to pray, we *can* be still before God, offering ourselves and our confusion to Him—knowing that no matter how we come to Him, we are acceptable in His sight as beloved sons.

For Thought and Discussion

1. Do your prayers tend to be generalized, or are they specific? If a child has concerns, do you think a loving father would want to hear his child express those needs specifically, or just in vague, broad terms?

2. If praying to God as "Father" is difficult for you, what other name or image of God is more helpful for you to keep in mind as you pray? Jesus? Lord? Holy Spirit? King? Creator? Savior? Master? Helper?

3. Is there a situation in your life right now about which you find it hard to pray? Perhaps it would help to write down at least the beginning of a simple prayer about your situation. This might enable you to begin to pray more specifically.

Praying for your Wife 6

As a single man, I sometimes prayed that God would give me a wife. Before I met Susan, my prayers went something like this:

"Lord, give me someone who is beautiful, bright, good ... and rich." When she came into my life, she surpassed most of the prayer. The *rich* part didn't matter anymore. I won't say that every moment of marriage has been a joy and a delight, but I have never for a moment regretted marrying her. It helps to remember that some pain and aggravation are part of how God matures us.

A wise man prays for his wife. He begins before he is married, before he even knows her, and he continues for the rest of his life. No other person is more central or more important in your life—and she always needs your prayers, even though she may not always tell you so.

Some women are pretty good at telling their husbands what they need or want. In fact, I have two different lists provided for me by my wife—one on my desk and another on my bureau. They remind me to: Repair the hallway wall. Fix the window box. Ask Bill about the bench. Call my mother. I need these reminders because—unfortunately—I can become preoccupied when Susan is talking. Or I get so caught up in my needs, I forget hers.

Early in his marriage, my friend Alf realized that he was not responding quite as quickly to his wife when she asked for his help as he had before they were married. He'd slipped into the habit of either ignoring her requests or delaying his response. He said it hit him one day that he was treating her less lovingly now that she was his wife than when she had been his fiancée—and that wasn't right. He made a resolution from that moment on always to do his best to respond immediately when she asked for his help. As I listened to Alf, I so admired the good sense and maturity of that resolution that I decided I'd try to do the same for Susan.

I have failed so completely that I doubt Susan even knows that I made that commitment. (But I will say in my defense that, as long as I am well-rested, in a good mood, not preoccupied, and have nothing else to do, I usually respond quickly when she asks for my help.)

Becoming a Praying Husband

Praying for your wife is as important as doing chores for her, buying gifts, or being attentive. It is, in fact, a way of *doing* for loved ones that you can fulfill anytime, anywhere. Even when your wife needs help in something that is beyond human ability, you can take that need to God on her behalf. And there is much in a family's life that is beyond our power to fix, arrange, or control.

These days, it seems like I'm praying every day for my children's safety as they travel. At this moment, one son is somewhere in the Pacific Northwest pedaling on a bicycle across America. A daughter is on her way to a tennis tournament several hours south of home. Another son is high up on a ladder painting a house. Someone else in the family is on an airplane, and another is in an automobile on a busy highway. Praying for their safety is an ongoing preoccupation of mine. But there's a lot more to praying for your family than that.

Discussing Your Needs Together

In May 1969, I sat beside my dad in the intensive care wing of our hometown hospital. I was single at the time and had come home from graduate school in New Jersey to see my dad because he had undergone serious surgery. Susan, who was working in Georgia, had come up to visit the family and me at the same time. In our conversation, Dad asked how she was doing. Then he squeezed my hand, looked into my eyes, and said, "Son, marry that girl."

That day we had what turned out to be our last conversation, and he had given me what would be his final bit of advice. He died unexpectedly two days later. I asked Susan that very day if she would become my wife.

Later that week, in the sad, shocking aftermath of Dad's sudden death, my young fiancée and I sat down to talk about our future. We decided to make a list of needs, questions, and decisions that we were concerned about. This became the beginning of our prayer list, which we used for several years to come.

I pulled out that little black vinyl notebook the other day and reviewed the many notations in Susan's handwriting and mine. They included a date, the request, and often another date, off to the side, with a brief description of how we had seen the prayer answered. One prayer was that Susan would find a job that was compatible with her gifts and experience. Less than a month later, she accepted an offer to be dean of women at a small private college—just the sort of thing we were hoping for. That first little notebook contains 88 entries of needs about which we prayed.

Now, almost 30 years later, I continue to pray for Susan. I'm still praying for our relationship—that it will continue to deepen and mature, that I will understand her better, that I will hear her more effectively, and serve her. I pray for her physical health to continue to be strong, and for her to be growing in peacefulness. I pray for her writing and teaching, and that we will always be able to talk together and have fun together.

In other words, *praying for your wife can become a way of life*. As her husband, you are her chief prayer warrior. This requires you to know her well and to stay tuned to her needs so you can pray wisely. You can pray *superficially* for your wife—or you can pray *significantly*. Let's consider some ways in which we can equip ourselves to pray significant, powerful prayers for our wives.

Spend Time Together

First, a man who wants to support his wife effectively through prayer must make time to be with her—to hear and understand her.

Before our children came along, it wasn't too difficult for Susan and me to maintain a close relationship. Even though we were both very busy with work and studies, we made a priority of going out together one night a week on a date. We'd talk about our concerns and cares. Then the children came along. They were under foot, so for many years we had a tradition called "tea time." When I got home from work, we'd sit together over a cup of tea and talk about our day. The children could be in the room, but they couldn't speak. Usually, we only managed 10 to 15 quiet minutes like this a day, but it enabled us to stay in touch.

Even if you travel a lot and are away from your family, you can make it a priority to stay in touch. Billy Graham, who has traveled as much as any of us, has always made a priority of telephoning his wife every day—no matter where he is around the world.

If you're going to pray for your wife, you've got to know what's going on in her life, what she's doing, what she's thinking, what she's feeling. This can take a good deal of thoughtfulness and attention on our part. Your wife may not tell you everything that's on her mind. She may be burdened about a child, or fearful for a parent, but not be able to talk about it. You may have to gently draw it out of her with patient questions. She may have some dreams and desires that are too personal or difficult to talk about. She may be hurting, having been wounded by a friend or beaten down emotionally by someone, but she finds it too painful to talk about. A wise husband will make it a top priority to be with his wife and to talk to her. As the years go by he will learn to read her and to see beneath the surface. He will learn the right questions to help her open up. All of this helps him support her in prayer more effectively.

Look for Purposes, Patterns, and Priorities in Her Life

I ask God to show me the major priorities, patterns, and purposes in Susan's life. It's helpful for me to distinguish between the day-to-day concerns and the more long-term, overarching prayers. *Therefore, once or twice a year I prepare a formal list of items that I pray about all year long on behalf of my wife.* Traditionally, I go to a place where I can be alone for a significant amount of time and I think about her needs as I know them. I look at Susan's life from several different angles—physical, mental, emotional, social, spiritual—and then I begin to list her needs.

For example, there may be two or three small physical problems that she's encountered—but which may actually indicate a change in her health. In her late 30's, as our children got a little older, I began to notice a growing concern in Susan's mind about her purpose in life. It was things like this that filled out my daily prayer list for her. Let me give you some more examples.

There is a sheet from my prayer notebook of six years ago that tells me I was praying for my wife to have a spirit of peace, a deepening sense of closeness to me, and more balance in her life between rest and activity, giving and receiving. At that time, I was praying for opportunities for her to develop her remarkable gifts of leadership and teaching. I prayed for her to find direction in an area of work she was interested in pursuing. I prayed for a physical problem she was having with her heart.

Here is another list from a few years earlier, in which I was praying for her ability to write three significant magazine articles that year—and for her involvement in a new women's ministry at the church.

Fifteen years ago I was praying that she would have peace during a time when she was so preoccupied with five small children that she was fighting to keep a sense of worth and a sense of hope for the future. I was praying for her to have a sense of personal progress in her life, and good times alone with each child. There was another prayer that God would teach her to accept herself more easily and not struggle with guilt.

As I look over the pages from the 1970s, '80s, and '90s, many of the prayers are the same, but I can also see a record of growth and change in my wife and in our marriage as well. It's a record of God's faithful responses to a loving husband who wanted to support his wife.

When I am considering my annual list of prayers for Susan, I ask myself questions like these:

◆ What are the concerns that she's most aware of in her life right now?

◆ What are issues of character that she's struggling with?

◆ What other relationships does she have in which she needs God's help now?

◆ What particular responsibilities is she dealing with now in which she needs God's help?

I find it's helpful to think about Susan's life from *her* point of view. For instance, how is she feeling about herself? How is she feeling about our relationship? How is she feeling about her future? What are the particular gifts, interests, and opportunities before her right now? Where does she need help as she plans for the future? What are her deep longings?

Sometimes when I'm praying for my wife, I try to see a mental image of her sitting with or standing before the Lord Jesus Christ. I imagine Him looking at her and I ask myself: What is He seeing? What is He saying? What is He seeking to do in her life? All of these questions help me formulate simple prayers to guide me as I pray for her in the most important and ongoing areas of her life.

Day-to-Day Prayers

In addition to these ongoing prayers, I bring to God the day-to-day situations in Susan's life. Over the years I've developed a sort of informal pattern in praying for her each morning.

It helps to consider the conversations we've had the night before and to ask myself questions: What's on her mind today? What is on her agenda for today? What is she likely to be feeling? What burdens and apprehensions will she have? What responsibilities and pressures confront her today? What is she anticipating with excitement? What things will challenge her?

Then I pray not just for her, but for the people she will be with, and I try to remember the specific things that she might need God's help with during that day. Here are some examples:

- "Please give her an extra measure of peace, as she's apt to be worried about our son who is on the road today."

- "Please give her a love for _____ as she meets to talk with this woman about a problem in her life. Give her unusual insight as a counselor."

- "Help her to have the wisdom to know whether she should take advantage of the opportunity we discussed last night."

- "Help her to be able to trust that You will take care of this problem that we don't know how to deal with."

- "Please help her grow in her discipline to carry out those exercises the doctor recommended."

- "Please reassure her of my love for her and the children, even though I'm going to be away all week."

If I could personally meet these needs in Susan's life, there would be no need for me to ask God's help. And these needs represent only a few of the many concerns that a husband cannot necessarily handle. It only makes sense to ask God's help in these matters.

The Tough Places

Not every man has a happy marriage, and not every man has a wife for whom he finds it easy to be thankful day-by-day. His prayers might contain pleas to God to make certain changes in his wife—changes he can in no way make himself.

Every husband has to learn how far he can go in talking with his wife about things in her life that need to change, and when he must remain silent. The constructive criticism that we give and receive in marriage is a vital part of how we learn to grow and mature. But a wife is not always open to criticism, and sometimes our complaints are right, and sometimes unreasonable. If you can't talk with your wife or help her in the areas of her life that drive you crazy, certainly you can pray about them. If your wife has irritating habits or attitudes, it is possible that you—her husband, lover and supporter—are not the right person to bring about those changes in her life. But you can, as a prayer partner, work on these things by talking to God about them and seeking His help on her behalf.

◆ Bob's wife, for example, has a problem with explosive anger. Talking with her does little good, but he has seen her begin to mature in this area as he has prayed about it.

◆ Alec's wife has an unreasonable fear about dying from a painful disease. He prays regularly about this fear and has seen God give her peace.

◆ Lewis' wife doesn't seem to care about her appearance. He prays for divine wisdom, asking how he can strengthen her self-image to the point where she will care about how she looks.

Chapter 6: Praying for Your Wife

Wives *can* change. They *can* mature; they *can* heal. I've seen it happen again and again. Praying for change in your wife is not an idle prayer. And sometimes such a prayer has to begin with praying for your wife's *husband*, who has problems of his own! (But that's another matter, which we'll examine later.)

Sometimes we men can be abrasive and abusive in pointing out our wife's flaws. And certainly we can talk maturely about what's bothering us or a need we see. But praying is better yet, and more productive.

Praying With Scripture

There are many passages of Scripture that can be helpful to us in praying for our wives—passages of assurance and promise that we can use as guides.

For instance, if your wife is preoccupied with anxieties or depression, let Paul's words in Philippians 4:4-7 guide your prayers for her:

> May she rejoice in the Lord always. Let Your gentleness give her a sense of the presence of the Lord. Help her not be anxious about anything, but to know You hear her as she prays. Help her to present her requests to You, O God, and then give her the peace of God that transcends all understanding, to guard her heart and her mind.

Suppose she's in danger, or ill, or afraid. Turn to Psalm 23 and let it guide you in your prayer for her:

> Give to her a sense that You, Lord, are her Shepherd, and that You will not leave her in need. Give her a sense of well-being and quietness. Restore peace to her soul. Walk with her through each valley, helping her to fear no evil, giving her assurance that You, O Lord, are with her. Touch her with Your Holy Spirit, and give her an awareness of Your goodness and love, which follows her step by step.

Suppose she has sinned or made some mistake in judgment for which she is sorry and has asked God's forgiveness but still feels troubled with guilt. Turn to Psalm 103 and convert it into a prayer for her:

Dear Father, help her to be reminded of Your goodness in forgiving her sins. Give her a sense of Your compassion and graciousness—that You are slow to anger and abounding in love. Remind her that You do not treat her as her sins deserve, or repay her according to her iniquities, but that Your love for her is so great that You have removed her transgressions from her. Help her to see You as a loving Father who has compassion for His children. Remind her that You know that she is made of dust and bound to fail, but that from everlasting to everlasting your love for her is constant.

Perhaps this prayer, adapted from Ephesians 3:14-20, is appropriate for your wife:

I kneel before You, Father, and pray that out of Your glorious riches You may strengthen her in her inner being, so that Christ may dwell in her heart through faith. I pray that she, being rooted and established in Your love, may grasp how wide and long and high and deep is the love of Christ and know His love that surpasses knowledge. Fill her completely with the fullness of Your love. Give to her an overwhelming sense of Your power, which is able to do immeasurably more than she can ask or imagine, so that she may have peace and joy.

The promises in the Bible have been written for God's people to cling to when in need. Rely on these promises in prayer on your wife's behalf, and ask God to fulfill particular promises for her. Consider the following passages that you may adapt in your prayers:

Discouragement

Be of good courage, and He shall strengthen your heart … hope in the Lord (Psalm 31:24, KJV).

Wait on the Lord; Be of good courage, and He shall strengthen your heart; Wait, I say, on the Lord (Psalm 27:14, NKJV)!

Worry

You will keep in perfect peace [her] whose mind is steadfast, because [she] trusts in you (Isaiah 26:3, NIV).

My God shall supply all your needs according to His riches in glory in Christ Jesus (Philippians 4:19, NASB).

If that is how God clothes the grass of the field, which is here today and tomorrow is thrown into the fire, will He not much more clothe you … ? So do not worry, saying, `What shall we eat?' or `What shall we drink?' or `What shall we wear?' … your heavenly Father knows that you need [these things] (Matthew 6:30-32, NIV).

Loneliness

I will not leave you comfortless: I will come to you (John 14:18, KJV).

Nothing in all creation can separate us from the love of God in Christ Jesus our Lord (Romans 8:39, NEB).

Dissatisfaction

My people shall be satisfied with My goodness, declares the Lord (Jeremiah 31:14, NASB).

And you shall have plenty to eat and be satisfied, and praise the name of the Lord your God, Who has dealt wondrously with you (Joel 2:26, NASB).

[God] satisfies the longing soul, and fills the hungry soul with goodness (Psalm 107:9, NKJV).

Confusion

I will instruct you and teach you in the way you should go. I will guide you with my eye (Psalm 32:8, NKJV).

God is not the author of confusion but of peace (1 Corinthians 14:33, NKJV).

Whether you turn to the right or to the left, your ears will hear a voice behind you, saying this is the way, walk in it (Isaiah 30:21, NIV).

Impatience

Wait on the Lord: Be of good courage, and He shall strengthen your heart. Wait, I say, on the Lord (Psalm 27:14, NKJV).

The fruit of the Spirit is love, joy, peace, patience, kindness, goodness, faithfulness, gentleness, self control (Galatians 5:22, RSV).

Grief

Blessed are they that mourn: for they shall be comforted (Matthew 5:4, KJV).

Blessed be the God and Father of our Lord Jesus Christ, the Father of mercies and God of all comfort; who comforts us in all our afflictions (2 Corinthians 1:3-4, NASB).

These are just a few of the promises God has made to His people in Scripture. Our role as husbands is to sometimes go to God on our wife's behalf and share her need, asking Him to keep His promise to her.

Praying With Her

One of the most important yet daunting things we can do for our wives is to pray *with* them. For a few men this is easy; for most it is difficult. Some would sooner do almost anything than approach their wives about praying together.

Perhaps you feel inadequate. Maybe you find it embarrassing to pray out loud with another person. Whatever your reason, it is well worth trying to overcome your hesitancy. Let me make some simple suggestions.

1ST *START SMALL AND KEEP IT SIMPLE.* You might say something like: "I've been thinking it might help our home life if we could sometimes pray together. I know it might be awkward at first, and I'm certainly not any kind of spiritual giant. But what if, say, at the end of breakfast we take a few minutes and have a simple prayer together to start our day?"

Or you might suggest, "I'm thinking that just before we go to sleep, it might be a good thing for us to turn to God in prayer together and ask His help with the things that we're facing. I'd like to try that if it's all right with you."

2ND *STICK TO THE FOLLOWING GUIDELINES:* Be brief. Use natural words. Don't try to be religious or super-spiritual. Take the lead, and show that you are taking prayer seriously. Be practical—pray about everyday matters that are of concern to your family.

3RD *BE WILLING TO TALK TO GOD—WITH YOUR WIFE PRESENT— ABOUT YOUR RELATIONSHIP WITH HIM.* Thank God for His gifts, blessings, and answers to prayer. Confess your sins—don't hesitate to ask God to forgive you when you need to. Ask for His help.

Praying for Your Wife's Husband

Ask yourself: What does my wife really need in a husband? What things does she need from me? What qualities does she need to see exhibited in my life? Then pray that God will begin developing these qualities in you.

The following prayer is one I pray for my wife's husband from time to time:

> *Father in heaven, help me to be the man my wife needs me to be today. I know that I cannot meet her every need—only You can do that—but help me to always be caring and attentive toward her. Help me to be sensitive to her concerns and to provide for her as I ought. Enable me to listen to what she says, and to always be courteous and thoughtful toward her and encouraging to her in all her efforts. Help me always to be alert to protect her, and defend her against harm or insult. Please give me the will and energy to share my heart and my thoughts with her, and to tell her the things that seem obvious and self-evident to me but may not be clear to her at all. Help me to be kind, appreciative, and fun to live with. Amen.*

Praying About the Things You Dislike in Her

It is no accident that you are married to this particular woman—and it is no accident that she is the way she is. This doesn't mean that everything about her is as it ought to be—but God has allowed this woman, as she is, to be in your life for some very good reasons.

Years ago, when Susan and I had not been married very long, I was still trying to figure out what it meant to be a minister of God. I found that from time to time I was threatened by certain gifts that Susan possessed. For instance, she has an unusual ability to organize, and she communicates effectively. She could outline a talk or message much more easily than I could. Sometimes, without any effort on her part, entire sermons came into her mind and she wrote them down and gave them to me. I was still in seminary trying to figure out how to communicate well, and I found this more than a little annoying. I was supposed to be the minister, but my wife seemed to have more gifts in this area than I did! This was true in other areas too. And I found myself actually resenting her from time to time.

One day when I was mulling this over during a quiet period, it seemed that God was reminding me that He had given me Susan to help me to be more useful for His purposes—with gifts that would help me to be more effective than if I were on my own. He reminded me that I had strengths she did not have, and that she needed me as much as I needed her: "I've made you both this way and brought you together—so be thankful and *stop being critical.*"

Most often it's not our wife's *gifts* that bother us, though. No woman is perfect, and we can easily become focused on our wife's flaws. A negative focus will crush all desire to pray for your spouse—unless you actively work to change your spirit and attitude.

Reversing Your Negative Spirit

In her book *Thirty-One Days of Praise,* Ruth Myers includes two prayers that I find particularly helpful in turning around my attitude toward people when I've become too critical or when I'm having a hard time seeing the good. Whenever you get focused on your wife's flaws, consider these words:

> *Father, I thank You for the people in my life who seem to bring more pain than joy, for I believe You have let our paths cross for*

important reasons. Thank You for the good things You want to do in my life through the things that bother me. (Their irritating habits? Moodiness? Unloving ways? Demands? Insensitivity? Unrealistic expectations?) I'm grateful that You are with me to meet my needs ... even when those close to me fail to do so. I'm so glad that You are also within me working to make me more like Jesus—more patient, more gentle, more loving— through the very things I dislike.

Thank You, too, that You love these people and that your love is adequate to meet their deepest needs and to transform their lives.

And so, though I may not feel grateful, I give thanks for them by faith.... Thank You that by Your power I can receive them as You receive me—just as I am, warts and wrinkles and hang-ups and all…. Help me choose not to judge but to forgive them ... to cancel any debts I think they owe me—apologies, obligations ... Through Your grace, I choose to wipe clean any slate of grievances I have within me and to view these people with a heart that says, "You no longer owe me a thing."

Thank You for Your Spirit, who empowers me so that I can do them good, delight in You, and commit my way to You, resting in You as you unfold Your good purposes in these relationships—in Your time.

Thank You, Lord, for each specific strong point and admirable quality in my life partner. Thank You for bringing us together, and for the way Your love sweetens our earthly love! I bless You, Lord, for the many benefits You have given me through this dear one. Here are some special reasons I want to thank You for our relationship: [add your reasons][1]

Myers also recommends that we begin to pray and thank God for the *specific weakness* or *failures* of the people close to us, such as our wives. Focus your prayers in praise to God that He is powerful and well able to change your spouse, if and when He chooses.

In the meantime, remember that God is always at work to change you and me through the imperfections that frustrate us—if we will give ourselves completely into His hands to be shaped into the men He wants us to be.

For Thought and Discussion

1. If your parents prayed for each other, what impact do you think this had on your home?

2. In what ways have you found it helpful to get a better understanding of your wife's deeper, more personal concerns?

3. What actions will you take to pray more thoughtfully and consistently for your wife?

4. What one important prayer will you begin to pray for your wife? Attempt now to express it simply and specifically.

1. Ruth Myers, *31 Days of Praise* (Sisters, Ore.: Multnomah Books, 1994), pp.88-89.

Praying for your Children 7

I have a great friend who is to me the image of a "man's man." Larry Roadman was an all-star athlete in college, a platoon leader in Vietnam, a marine recruiter at places like Berkeley in the Vietnam era—and also a world traveler, farmer, skier, and a successful international businessman. And now, he is the father of two sons. He married Betsy a little later in life, and maybe that's the cause of his unusual gratitude for his wife and children. It's this deep gratitude that has made Larry one extraordinary dad. He does more for and with his sons than any father I've known.

For years, Larry has maintained an important practice regarding his family. Early each morning, before they wake up, he stands at the bedroom doors of each one and prays for them individually. "Praying for them is probably the single most important thing I do for them," says Larry.

He's right. *Praying* for our children is every bit as important as playing with them, instructing them, and providing for them.

Do you pray for your children? At all? Regularly? Would you like to develop the habit of praying for them more?

I like the prayer of another man I know who prays each morning for his children:

Lord, may Your blessing rest upon each one. May they know Your care, provision, peace, guidance, and Your overwhelming goodness. May they always be firm in their commitment to You and to one another. May they each fulfill a significant mission for You, growing up in all ways into Your fullness. May they know my love for them and the utmost privilege I have to be their father. May we have, by your grace, all of eternity to grow in the love that we have begun to experience here and now. Amen.

Becoming a Praying Dad

How should a man pray for his children?

Perhaps the best way I can help you in this area is to show you how I have grown as a praying dad—letting you in on some of the specific prayers I've prayed for the changing needs of one of my children.

Just before my daughter Allison was married, we had several good long father—daughter talks about things that were important to us. In one of those conversations, she asked me if one day she could have the battered and taped-up old copy of Oswald Chambers' *My Utmost for His Highest*, the daily devotional book that I've read and carried around with me ever since I was a college student. She said that her earliest and most meaningful memories of me are of my being in the study early in the morning, praying for her and the rest of the family. She told me how secure she had felt to know that her dad was praying early every day for all of them.

In that week before her wedding, I pulled out some old notes that I'd saved through the years, and I reviewed some of the prayers I'd prayed for her since she was a small child.

Here are some of the prayers I prayed when she was about two-years old:

◆ That she would learn how to take responsibility

◆ That she would be confident, honest, and quiet when needed

◆ That God would be molding her husband-to-be into a man after His own heart

◆ That she would know me, her dad, and love me—and for our relationship to be especially close

A year or so later, my notes show that I was praying in the following ways for her:

◆ That she would not see and hear the ugly things of the world until she was able to handle them emotionally and spiritually

◆ That she would not have an overly sensitive conscience

When she was four, I see that I spent four months praying that she would have a better appetite at mealtimes. (That prayer was marked throughout with double checks at the end of the line.) I prayed also that she would have excellent eyesight and not have to wear glasses. (That prayer was answered eventually with a loving *no* from God.) Then I prayed that she would be more outgoing.

When she was five, I prayed for her manners to improve. At six, I prayed for her to develop more of a curious nature and not to be too inhibited. At age seven, I asked God to guide us in our reading together, to books that would thrill and teach her—and also to help Susan and me discern what caused her difficulty with allergies (or that she would be healed of them).

By the time she was 12, I prayed that she would excel in tennis … find some special Christian friends … that she'd be learning God's truths, and learning to express her own ideas. (I was still praying that her allergies would be overcome. In fact, I still pray that prayer today!)

My prayer notes go on and on. Now I'm praying for Allison and her husband, Will, who are into their third year of marriage. I pray that she will keep a balanced life, for her teaching career—and particularly I pray for her relationship with Will as they establish priorities that can lead to a rich, strong, long life together. And I pray for my son-in-law and his work as a youth minister at a church in Florida.

As I look over these briefly written notes recorded over the last 25 years, I'm amazed and overwhelmed at the goodness of God in answering my prayers for my daughter. Here is a record of her life, of my concern for her, but most of all of God's faithfulness in taking care of her. These lists are a treasure to me.

So, where do *you* begin?

Start Early

I'll bet that, by now, I've made the point with you about prayer lists, notebooks, and journals. The point is, really, that it pays in many ways to keep a written record of God's faithfulness and your own, and of the growth of your family. A notebook or a journal is a good tool, a regular reminder to you if it's used well. And it's more than that—it's a wonderful, powerful reminder to our children, later in life, of God's faithfulness to them.

I recommend that you begin to pray regularly for your children *now*. Start *today*.

I began praying for each of my children from the time they were conceived. And the moment we got home from the hospital, Susan and I laid each tiny newborn on our bed, got down on our knees, and thanked God for this child. We dedicated him or her to God for His purposes. And we begged His help! As soon as our eldest came home from the hospital, I began a habit I continued with all the rest. I would slip into the room of each one just after they had gone to sleep. I'd sit on their bed, lay my hand on their forehead and ask God's blessing upon them.

My kids are grown now and stay up much later than I do. But when the kids were young, either their mother or I would try to pray with them at bedtime. Our prayers with them were usually brief and dealing with concerns in their own lives. We prayed for simple things like their being able to stop wetting the bed, not having bad dreams, and learning to ride a bike. We prayed for their friends in need, about fears, to be chosen for a team, etc. The children learned to pray for themselves and for one another as we led them in prayer times like these.

One night, I was praying with my son Chris after his first day at school in the first grade. Both his sister and brother had prayed for him the night before that he would make friends. Now they were anxious to know if he'd hooked up with anybody. We were overjoyed to find out he had. And now he wanted prayer for the next small dilemma. He was a little disappointed because he thought school would be more "grown-up" than it was: "All we did today was color!"

We have never sugarcoated our approach to prayer when talking to our children. We've never made God out to be Santa Claus, or a mechanical miracle-dispenser. He can say *yes, no,* or *wait* in answer to our prayers. When God seems to be silent, we talk openly about that, and about what His purposes might be in remaining silent or in making us wait. When our prayers have been answered, we've called it to our kids' attention to *remind* them of God's goodness.

Show Them That Prayer Is Important

The natural way to teach our children to turn to God and ask for help is by showing them *we* believe prayer is real. When your child is overwhelmed by some fear, disappointment, or frustration, *gently* take a moment to pray about it. Before some event that is of concern to your child—say, a new experience at school, an athletic event, a job interview, or a crisis with a friend—make it a point to pray with your son or daughter.

It has always been our custom as a family, when we're in the car about to leave home on a long trip, to pray and ask God's protection. But recently I was reminded that it's important to give God thanks at the end of a trip as well.

I had the opportunity to spend time in East Africa with a Kenyan bishop and his family. One day, we left their home to travel up into the highlands around Mt. Kenya in order to visit a congregation. It was a rugged area. Before we left, the bishop led us in a prayer asking God's protection. At the end of the day we returned absolutely exhausted. When we pulled into the yard and the engine was turned off, I immediately opened my door to get out. Then I hesitated. No one else was moving, so I sat back, waiting. After a few moments, the bishop's wife said quietly, "I think we'll pray now." Then she led the family in thanking God for His care, protection, and mercy throughout the day. As our children see us make a priority of reaching out to the Lord for help, or offering Him thanks, they learn how important this is in our lives, and we help them to grow in awareness that God is their good, caring Father.

I've already mentioned our many prayer journals. One of them has always sat near the breakfast table, and in it we've recorded some of our family's needs. Most of the requests are recorded in the handwriting of one child or another. When I look through the pages, I'll find a prayer for an uncle to sell his house. Our prayers for another family to have a baby. One of my daughter's prayers for one of her friends to get a date for homecoming—and then there are prayers for Uncle Fitz and all his friends to be kept safe from Hurricane Hugo. Many times, we prayed together for wars and conflict to end.

Probably the most traditional time to pray with children is at mealtime or at bedtime. The other day a dad told me that he's still praying at bedtime with his son who is now a teenager. He uses that as the main time during the day to connect with his son. Even though he has to work hard at organizing his schedule so that he can be home at his children's bedtime, he's tried to make it a priority because the commitment has given them so much in terms of bonding, spiritual growth, and instruction.

Sitting on the edge of your son's or daughter's bed, in a relaxed mood, is a great way to listen to them talk about how they've spent their day. A wise father will be there, ask a few leading questions, and then *listen*. Your primary goal is not to lecture, to correct, or to preach. It is to listen—then to pray and help lift the burdens of the day and refocus your child's spirit and mind on God as they come to rest.

Knowing HOW to Pray for Our Children

When our children were still pretty young, Susan and I developed the habit of getting away in August, before school started, for an overnight alone. During that time we would talk seriously about each of our children. We wanted to try to begin the new school year with a common understanding of their needs. Susan was usually far more aware of their needs because she was with them so much more of the time. (One year I was able to take a summer of sabbatical leave, and we spent that summer together as a family away from home. I found at the end of that summer, during which I had been with my children all day every day, that I was as fully aware of their needs as Susan was.) Your ability to discern the needs of your family members is directly proportional to the amount of time you spend with them.

The needs and concerns that Susan and I discussed formed my conversation with God on behalf of each child for that following year. One year, Susan was particularly concerned that our younger son, Chris, was getting lost in the midst of our five children. He always seemed to be left out. He was also close in age to his demanding little twin sisters. Susan felt that he needed to feel special, and so we began to pray that somehow he would begin to know just how important he was.

Months later, Chris, who was about 11 at the time, had a terrible accident. He was swinging on a high bar and fell headfirst onto the cement below. The injury was serious, and he was hospitalized for some time. Finally, he was released and, on the way home, he and Susan were discussing all that he'd been through. What impressed him most was this: From the moment he'd recovered consciousness, scores of people had been to see him, and they'd showered him with love. One college boy who had visited Chris had told him he had a strong sense that God had some special purpose for Chris' life. As he reflected on these things, Chris said, "I think the one thing I've learned from all this, that I never really knew before, is just how special I am—and how many people love me and believe in me."

In a strange and unexpected way, God had answered our prayer for this little boy.

When our eldest was about 12, we started a new tradition. We asked our children to join with us in thinking about their needs for the coming year. We asked each of them to sit by themselves for a while and think about the different areas of their life—school, sports, friends, church. Then they were to share with us their personal hopes, dreams, concerns, and needs for the new school year. Although they reacted predictably *against* this sort of thing in the early years, eventually they got used to the idea. Now they have developed the pattern in their own lives of sitting down every autumn and going through the process in advance of our family's "annual needs and goals meeting." It's become that important to all of us.

Three Simple Principles

A wise parent learns several simple principles early on.

1ST *DON'T DO FOR YOUR KIDS WHAT THEY CAN DO FOR THEMSELVES.* When they're old enough to dress themselves, you encourage them to do it. When they're old enough to fix their own lunch—or call a coach for information, or earn money—you let them do it. This builds independence and a sense of self-worth.

2ND *EVERY LOVING PARENT PROVIDES FOR THE NEEDS OF HIS CHILDREN AS BEST HE CAN.* This doesn't mean that we *can* or *should* give them everything they want. We need to teach them the difference between wants and needs. We need to teach them that, often, you have to cope in life with less than what you'd like to have—in finances, health, friendships, success. This begins to build a sense of the reality of life, and the habit of finding contentment in whatever circumstance you find yourself. There are many, many things that no one can do for their child.

 AND MOST IMPORTANT—A WISE PARENT REALIZES THAT WE ASK GOD TO DO FOR THEM THE THINGS THAT WE, OR THEY, CANNOT DO FOR THEMSELVES. For instance, you can train your child in the difference between right and wrong. And you can work hard to instill the habits of self-discipline and patience. But there are matters of the heart and facets of moral character that you can't transfer to a child. You can talk about and model the quality of compassion, but you can't *produce* it in your child's heart. You can't give your child a lighthearted nature or a peaceful spirit. Sure, there are a lot of things you can do to give your child *opportunities* to grow in these directions, but in the end these things need the help of God in order to develop. So while a loving parent is working hard to feed, clothe, discipline, and build self-confidence and a sense of direction in his child, at the same time he's praying that God will help him in these areas, and that God will develop in each child qualities like moral virtue, purity, enthusiasm, vision, imagination and creativity, courage, selflessness, and wisdom in solving conflicts.

As parents, we learn to pray that God will bless our efforts and help our children to learn their lessons well—and that they will learn to hear His voice for themselves.

Not long ago, one of our sons called from college to ask our guidance on a major decision: should he serve on the school honor court, or should he take a job on the editorial board of the college daily newspaper? We honestly didn't know what was the right thing for him to do. We went over the pros and the cons of both with him as best as we could discern and understand them. But now it was up to him to try his own wings as a son of the heavenly Father. We assured him we'd pray for him to have wisdom in making the right choice.

How good it was to know that this young man knew how to pray and trust and wait for confidence and right direction to come.

There are things going on in the life of your child every day for which he or she needs God's guidance and care. The closer you are to your child, the more able you will be to pray wisely and transfer the value of prayer.

A Prayer for My Children's Father

Here is a prayer you might use as you commit yourself to the task of being a praying dad:

Help my children's father today, Lord, to be observant of them and sensitive to them. Give me unusual insight into their lives. Help me to be secure in Your love and care, Father … for I need Your help as much as they do.

Help me give attention to my children and be available to them to give guidance in the decisions they face. Help me to provide a moral foundation for them. Help me to give them emotional health by valuing and caring for them.

Help me to provide for their financial needs, and to prepare them for the world they'll face as they grow. Help me to share my relationship with You, Father.

And today, Lord, remind me to take the time to understand my children's perspectives before I speak. Remind me to be more playful with them again.

Give me the grace, Lord, to model for my children what it means to be a good and a godly person. Amen.

For Thought and Discussion

1. If there were three prayers you'd like to see answered this year in your children's lives, what would they be?

2. Where and when is it most natural for you to establish a habit of praying with your children? Will you take the initiative to begin doing this now?

3. What can you do to learn more about your children's concerns and hopes?

Praying for Yourself 8

If you read through the New Testament, you will see that Jesus spent a good portion of His prayer time praying for Himself. We tend to think that praying for oneself is a selfish thing that is to be avoided. But if the Son of God Himself had to seek the heavenly Father's help and guidance, how *much more* do we? In fact, if we are praying in humility, wanting to become godly men and servants to our families, our prayers will help us to center our lives in God—and that's exactly what praying is ultimately supposed to do. Although this book is about praying for your family, I hope you've picked up that the subtext is on how we hear from and cooperate with God in His work of caring for the people He has entrusted to us.

I want to focus now on the man you are becoming, and some important aspects of your life that will only come to peace and stability when they become part of your relationship with God. In the early chapters of this book, we talked about various aspects of personal prayer. Now I want to give you specific, practical guidelines that can help you in praying for yourself and centering your life in an ongoing relationship with God.

Praying for Lifetime Concerns

When I was in my mid-thirties I began working on my own personal set of "governing principles." This was an attempt to establish in writing the chief concerns of my life, and to set out for myself my own personal ambitions—

not for my career, but for my character and relationships. I wanted to be clear about the kind of person I was trying to become. This list of principles has changed and enlarged slightly over the years and has become helpful to me in my personal prayer life.

Once a week, or thereabouts, it's become my custom to take some time to pray mainly for myself. I pray according to the principles that I want to govern my life for as long as I live. I know other men who do this, too.

Here is a list, prepared by one man I know, to show you what I mean:

1. *I want to love the Lord with all of my mind, heart, and strength.* May the praise of God, prayer, and acceptance of His answers characterize my life. May I seek to be with Him at all times and allow the Holy Spirit to fill me continually.

2. *I want to have the mind of Christ.* The will of God must be my highest priority. I seek to know God's Word, to love what He loves and hate what He hates. I seek to honor and please Him in all my relationships, commitments, and decisions. I commit myself to study and learn regularly from others who have walked closely with Him and to see myself as He sees me, caring more for God's approval than the approval of others.

3. *I want to show others how to follow Christ.* I want to be ready at all times to share Him with others. I want to be concerned with the growth of Christian friends—and especially my family. May I keep family time, and people time, high on my agenda—and to accept a place of authority in the lives of others as I mature.

4. *I want to love my wife and children as Christ loved the Church—* protecting and providing for them, encouraging their faith, caring for their health and the development of their gifts. I want to enjoy them, praise them, and always treat them with respect. May I prepare my children for whatever mission in life is theirs.

5. *I want to be a responsible, dependable man.* May I be a man of unquestioned integrity and purity of heart, a man who is growing in sound judgment … striving for justice … hungry for righteousness.

6. *I want to be kind to others.* May I be more thoughtfully, actively interested in other people. May I help them sense their value, expressing to them appreciation and gratitude when it is due. May I resist the temptation to criticize or gossip—and the temptation to leave the hard but necessary word unsaid. Make me strong enough to be a peacemaker who speaks the truth in love.

7. *I want to have the attitude of a learner.* I want to grow in knowledge, wisdom, and abilities. Times of solitude, time for study, and time with those wiser than I will be built into my life.

8. *I want to be humble and honest in self-appraisal.* May I never denigrate myself or others, but focus on what is praiseworthy in all people. I want to be patient with my own weaknesses, while challenging myself to growth in excellence.

9. *I want to live by faith* May I live by what God has said above all else. As I aim to grow in maturity and faith, I will commit only to worthy goals and dreams, which cannot be accomplished apart from God's help—and the help of others.

10. *I want to be determined, confident, and courageous.* May I be enthusiastic and unyielding in pursuing good things—also prayerful and patient when my goals are long in coming. Help me never to indulge in negative thoughts.

11. *I want to set excellence as the standard in my work.* May I organize well, commit to less, and make the best use of my time.

12. *I want to approach life with a sense of humor and a spirit of praise.* May I be fun to live with.

13. *I want to be careful with finances.* May I be thrifty but always generous to others. I want to get out of or stay out of unnecessary debt, and I want to tithe 10 percent and save 10 percent, with God's help.

14. *I want to maintain excellent health.* May I remember that my body is a temple of the Holy Spirit—may I be moderate in diet, faithful in exercise.

15. *I want a pure life.* I will not commit adultery. I will avoid lust in any form, and treat all women other than my wife as sisters or daughters. May I be alert to temptation of any kind and resist it, never listening to the devil's lies.

16. *I want to live my life here as a stranger.* May I not give final loyalty to earthly things, but to things that are eternal.

17. *I want to be a faithful friend.* May I keep in touch with those to whom I'm committed and who are committed to me.

18. *I want to know, develop, and multiply the gifts God has given me for His kingdom.*

19. *I want to honor the Sabbath principle.* May I rest regularly, so God can have the time to speak to me, and re-create me. No doubt you will develop similar principles by which you want to live. They should be lofty enough to stretch you but practical enough to be attained. It's right to ask God to help you be the best man you can possibly be. And to stay balanced, it's just as important to remember that all spiritual growth is a process—a lifetime journey. *Go gently with yourself.*

Making Covenants

Just as there are governing principles, there are certain covenants—or promises—that you may enter into. A promise both challenges and protects you. A *covenant* is, in fact, a solemn promise made between you and someone else under God. It's a commitment for life, made with the intention of giving yourself without reservation. Maybe it's a promise to your best friend to take care of his children should anything happen to him. It may be a promise to your son or daughter—to always be available whenever needed, no matter what. Your marriage vows are as serious as any covenant you will ever enter into. In these and other promises we make, we need the help and blessing of God in order to be faithful. Reviewing and praying through the covenants we enter into and the promises we make is a wise action for thoughtful men to take.

Just to illustrate this principle, I'll share with you one covenant that I made a few years ago about which I pray regularly. It's a solemn promise that I made to my wife, growing out of years of struggling with certain issues.

To the best of my ability, I will strive to hold to the following guidelines, because I want to ensure that I have the kind of family time I need. With God as my helper, I know this covenant will help me to live faithfully—and it will force me to grow in delegating responsibilities to others and to say *no* more often.

1. I will not commit to more than three nights away from home per week, including a night at the farm, unless Susan agrees that such a commitment is wise.

2. Each week I will not schedule more than two early meetings that will take me away from the family at breakfast time. I will do my best to take one of the girls out to breakfast each week as well.

3. If I'm away on Friday, I'll plan to be at home on Saturday afternoon from 1:00 on to be with the family.

4. I will plan to be home on Sunday afternoons.

5. I want to pray with you (Susan) each morning as well and will initiate this either before or after breakfast.

6. I will plan to have lunch with you every Tuesday and would like you to hold that time free. _____ has agreed to hold me accountable to these promises (Ecclesiastes 4:9-12; Proverbs 5:18).

Sometimes a man has to put his sacred honor on the line in such promises. If you do so, be forewarned: You're going to need God's help, *and* you'll need to make it a regular matter to pray for yourself.

Praying for Annual Concerns

Fresh challenges arise, and new opportunities present themselves with each passing year. You'll want to make these a matter of prayer too.

I have found it helpful to get away on an annual basis for a few hours, and to give thoughtful consideration to where I am and what my major concerns are for the upcoming year. I usually do this in August at about the same time Susan and I discuss our children's needs and we have our family "needs and goals" discussion. New Year's resolutions have never worked for me, so I develop a list of hopes, dreams, goals, and concerns, and share them with the family. Then I make it a matter of regular prayer. This has been tremendously beneficial to me. Here are some examples of the prayers I've offered for myself during our first few years of marriage:

◆ To be better at relating to all types of people

◆ To get over resenting interruptions

◆ To have a genuine love for the church staff and to express it so that they sense my love for them

◆ To care little what others think of me, and to care what God thinks

◆ To listen carefully to Susan and make her concerns my concerns

◆ To receive from God a right attitude toward conflict

When you ask God's help in matters like these, you'll be amazed to see the transformation that takes place in you over time as you progress toward becoming the man you want to be. In fact, you'll be overwhelmed at the faithfulness of God as He works in your life, and greatly encouraged to see yourself grow and change.

Praying for Day-to-Day Concerns

No matter how busy your life or how full your agenda, it's always possible to make at least *some* time to pray every day. If you are not able to carve out a quiet time for reflection, you can at least pray on the run. Even during short coffee or lunch breaks at work you can establish a prayer discipline.

Someone has said, "The earnest thoughts of a righteous man are considered as prayer unto God." I believe this is true when we invite God to speak to us and guide us, whenever we need to spend time in thoughtful consideration of problems or options. Acknowledge more frequently that God is present with you, and invite the Holy Spirit into your mind as you wrestle with decisions. All of one's daily life can be lived in the context of prayer, but our lives will be strengthened tremendously if we discipline ourselves to set aside time to pray and reflect each day.

No matter how restless, edgy, distracted, busy, or preoccupied you are, you *can* be still for more than 60 seconds and thoughtfully bring yourself into God's presence for a time of prayer. Stop making excuses, and do it! Fifteen to 20 minutes is not too much time, and the more you grow in your experience of prayer the more you'll want to set aside time. As many great men of prayer would tell you, "We're too busy *not* to pray."

If you would like help in establishing a structure for prayer, the following is one possible approach to your daily prayer time.

A Simple Approach to Daily Prayer

THANKS AND PRAISE. Begin by simply reflecting for a moment on the past 24 hours. You might thank God for any significant conversations, for good health or weather, for news from a friend, for the successful completion of a task. There are any number of things that will come to your mind if you'll only take a moment to recall the good things of the previous day.

One of the common courtesies that has been lost in our culture is that of saying thank you. People seem too busy to take the time to write a simple thank-you note or to telephone and express appreciation for a fine evening together. Not saying *thank you* to God, who is the giver of all good things, is the ultimate rudeness. Don't fall into this trap.

CONFESSION. As you think over the past day, ask God to show you if there is any way in which you have let Him or others down—anything for which you need to ask forgiveness. This is the hardest part of prayer for most men I know, but it results in the greatest growth as we learn to let the Holy Spirit convict us of our sins.

The word "confess" means, literally, "to agree with…." So confessing our sins to God means that we are simply agreeing with God about the things in our life that are wrong or hurtful and need to be changed. We're not telling God anything He doesn't already know—but maybe we need to admit these flaws to ourselves *and* recognize what we need to do to change or to pay back others where it's necessary. Honesty is what we need, for our part. God's mercy makes us clean.

ASK. Consider your schedule, appointments, tasks, decisions, the difficult matters before you, and anything else that's on your plate for the day. Offer it all up to God, asking His guidance and help. This is also a time in which God may speak to you if you'll let Him. Take time to consider, for instance, to think about the content of a particular conversation you'll be having—or your approach to a situation you'll face. As you ask God's help … *hesitate*. Wait and see if perhaps the Holy Spirit will nudge you in one direction or another. This "asking" time of prayer is when I also bring before God family members and their needs.

Bring your wife and children before God, asking His blessing and participation in the matters they are facing that day.

The great Old Testament prophet Samuel said to his friend Saul, *Far be it from me that I should sin against the Lord by failing to pray for you* (1 Samuel 12:23, NIV). And far be it from us that we should fail to pray for ourselves, as well as our families.

Today, commit yourself to a regular time daily, finding a quiet place to be alone. Commit yourself to grow in prayer. You will experience the help of God, and you will become more and more the man God wants to make you.

For Thought and Discussion

1. What are five to 10 governing principles that you want to be true of your life?

2. What areas have been sources of failure, shame, embarrassment, or discouragement in your life? How might you pray for changes and help in these areas?

3. For most of us, the list of shortcomings would be long! Remember that God is a loving, encouraging Father. Which areas of life would He want to *encourage* you in?

A Power Tool for Prayer 9

A screwdriver is a simple tool. It's also a powerful tool when it's used right. I want to tell you about a simple and powerful tool you can use to bring strength to your prayer life.

Most men have their own little personal inventory of essential items that they take with them whenever they're going to be away from home. We count as essential things like a razor, toothbrush, a clock, and a flashlight. Some men take along a couple of photos, and maybe a small portable coffeemaker. Two things I never fail to take with me are an old leather Bible and a skinny prayer notebook. For me, this notebook has become an invaluable, powerful tool.

Now, keeping a prayer notebook may strike you as too simple an idea to get really excited about. But the notebook itself is not the point: developing a daily, consistent lifestyle of prayer is what we're after. You could say that something as simple as a couple of round pieces of metal isn't a very exciting tool for building a good physique—and if you don't discipline yourself to use those barbells you *won't* develop muscles. But that's not the fault of the barbells, nor does it mean that they're not the right equipment for the job.

Sometimes the simplest tools are exactly right for the job. And in the matter of developing a lifestyle of praying for your family, a prayer notebook can be a powerful motivator, a record, and a device to challenge you to discipline yourself on those days when you think you're too busy or just "don't feel like" praying.

No, as men we don't need one more thing in our lives to make us feel guilty—like a prayer notebook staring us in the face, as if to ask, "Why haven't you written in me lately, pal?" Let's agree, right now, to push guilty feelings aside whenever we're inconsistent in praying for our families. Guilt is a lousy motivator. But let's *do* commit to some method of learning the discipline of prayer, until it becomes as natural and enjoyable as it is meant to be.

Organizing Your Thoughts

When I was about 18 or 19 I began to realize that there were more situations and people that I needed to pray for than I could keep track of. So I got one of those black-and-white school composition books and began jotting down the names of people in various situations and using it as a reminder. Now, when you hit on an idea that's helpful, you don't want to let it go. Over the years I have consistently followed this pattern—experimenting a little here and there with different approaches, different types of books—but I've stuck with the basic idea *because it worked.* For me, the secret has been in capturing concerns—whether mine or Susan's or the children's—and having a simple way to remind myself that I need to hold these matters before God.

Because I'm a pastor, I suppose more people ask me to pray for them than could be said of most people. If the circumstances allow me to pray right there on the spot, I will pray there and then and not wait. But if I'm not able to do that, I try to jot a quick note on a piece of paper and stick it in my pocket. That night when I'm pulling off my shirt I'll run across it and put it on my desk, next to my prayer notebook. The next morning when I'm spending some time in prayer it will bring to my mind the situation.

Sometimes I'll write it down in my notebook—if it's something that I want to faithfully pray about. If it's a temporary situation I'll pray then and move on.

As I've said, this prayer notebook idea can be as simple as you want it to be. My approach has become more highly organized, but that's just because I've been refining it for so many years. I don't know many men who couldn't benefit from a more disciplined approach to prayer, but do what works for you. As I pass on my methods, feel free to use the ideas that appeal to you, or adapt my thoughts to your way of doing things.

A Notebook Divided Into Daily Sections

Get yourself a handy, compact, loose-leaf notebook made of vinyl or leather or something durable. It's been helpful for me to use the kind of notebook that has storage slots on the inside of the front and back covers because this is a good place to slip special notes that I want to save.

Using dividers, make a section marked *Daily*, and then make sections for each day of the week. Put some plain, unlined, durable paper in each section. Instead of having a different slot for Saturday and Sunday, you may want to do what I do and have a slot marked *Weekends*. The dividers need to be strong enough to last. (I find that I change books every three to four years, but I change the contents substantially on an annual basis.)

Photographs

Many years ago I noticed that photographs were particularly important to me. They helped me to focus more effectively on the people whose picture I was observing, and they brought back memories of special times in the past. So I decided to use photographs in my prayer notebook as a way of helping me concentrate more intently on the persons for whom I was praying. As a result, my notebook is full of photographs and notes written in my own handwriting at various times. The thing wouldn't win any awards for neatness or appearance, but it fits with my needs and that's the point.

Focus

If you try this method, you will probably find that you can only focus on a few needs or concerns each day with any real interest or intensity.

There are *some* people and things you will no doubt want to pray about unfailingly every day, like the chronic illness of your wife or child, the ongoing job stress you are living with, the child who is struggling through school, the son or daughter whose marriage is strained. In my own *Daily* section, I have two or three pictures of my entire family, a prayer I pray for my children every day, a list of things I pray about for my wife every day, a picture of my mom and my siblings, and a few personal items. (I also include four pictures of other people for whom I'm personally committed to pray every day—a woman and her child in western Kazakstan, a Russian Orthodox priest in Moscow, the African bishop and his wife in Kenya, and family friends from our church who live in Nairobi.) In addition, I've got a couple of pages with photos of all of my godsons and goddaughters, along with reminders to pray for them. Though some of the people and situations that go into this *Daily* category will change, it will always contain my immediate family and godchildren.

On the *individual days* of the week, I have a sheet or two devoted to one of my children specifically. Typically, there's a date and then a note on what I'm praying about. If the time comes when I sense that the prayer has been completely answered, I mark a line through it and write down the fulfillment.

Many prayers for your family will be continued from year to year as you update your notes each year, but expect the list to change significantly.

Often, I use pictures of my wife and children that have a special significance. For instance, when I'm praying for one of my sons, I might have a photo of him with a close friend, because I want to remember to pray for his close relationships. Or I might have a picture of my daughter taken at school or on the athletic field, similarly, as a reminder of major areas of her life that are her highest concerns. I like a picture of my mother that was taken with my twin daughters on the front steps of the ancestral family home in Raleigh, N.C.—the place has now passed out of the family, but it reminds me of our family heritage, for which I give thanks.

I find that I prefer to replace the photos of family members frequently. With other folks, I might still be using a photo that is several years old. (This is a great way to use those photographs that people send out with annual letters at Christmastime.)

The main point is to use this, or any other means, to keep your attention focused. For me, having a photograph to look at is all the reminder I need to keep my head in the game.

Family vacation is a good time to update a notebook like this—or else one of those long, rainy weekends. It takes a little time and it's easy to put off, even though you mean to do it. My custom is to devote a block of time to it around Labor Day weekend, after we've had plenty of time as a family through the summer to talk about our needs and goals for the upcoming year. (The end of summer usually affords lots of good family photos, maybe more so than at any other time of the year.)

Make the Idea Work for You

If you decide to try this idea, don't think it's something that you must slavishly follow. *It's simply an aid.*

When I sit down alone in the morning, I find that usually I want to talk to the Lord quietly about other things before I open my prayer notebook. My pattern goes something like this:

First, I recall events and circumstances of the last day—thanking God for the things for which I'm grateful and for particular blessings over the last 24 hours. Next comes a brief time of self-examination in which I consider my need to do business with God about sin in my life. Then I consider the day before me, the main demands that are weighing on me. I pray for myself and commit myself to God's care and direction.

Then, I pray for Susan and each of my children, remembering before God any particular concerns that are appropriate for them individually that day. I do the same for my mother and my siblings.

After that, I pull out the prayer notebook. I turn first to the *Daily* section and pray for those general concerns and character items that I've committed to pray for every day—as well as the other people for whom I pray on a daily basis. Finally, I turn to the section devoted to that particular day of the week and pray for the people and situations included there.

My own personal discipline includes turning to Scripture for a time of reading and study. Sometimes I will turn to the Bible before I pull out the prayer notebook. Some days I don't use the notebook at all.

For me, this little notebook has become a kind of sacred thing. It's a book that reminds me of the people and goals that are of greatest value to me and, I believe, to God. If the house were burning, these notebooks are among the few things I would retrieve. I keep my old ones together on a particular section of one shelf in the house, and find that several times during the year I feel the need to go to one of these old notebooks for one reason or another—say if I want to remind myself, Susan, or one of the children how God worked specifically in the past.

> *These notebooks become a record of our spiritual journeys and the mighty acts of God.*

When all is said and done, this simple "power tool" can become one place to keep together your hopes, dreams, and concerns—not just for yourself but for the people who are most important in your life. It can help in developing the discipline of prayer. Just sitting on your desk, it's a great reminder, and once you pick it up it becomes a guide, helping you to bring order to this challenging area of our lives. It gives me a sense that I'm being responsible in this crucial area of my life. As I've said, these notebooks also become a record of our spiritual journeys *and* the mighty acts of God. The prayer notebook becomes an overwhelming record of events and concerns in the lives of all the special people in your life, and whenever you pull down an old one and look through it, you will find yourself giving thanks to God for the way He's worked in one situation after another.

Think for a moment. What would it mean to your own children one day in the future to have a written account of their father's prayers for them? You can bet that your prayer notebook will become a cherished and valuable record for them. Isn't that the kind of spiritual heritage you want to leave for your family?

For Thought and Discussion

1. If you could begin a discipline suggested by the author in this chapter, what impact would it have on your prayer life? Will you do it? When will you set aside time to begin working on your prayer notebook?

2. Write out a personal prayer now for your wife or for your children.

Prayers for Busy Men 10

The more you learn about prayer, the more you realize that we are talking about more than asking and getting. We are talking about growing in a deeply personal, intimate friendship with God—one that expresses itself in many ways.

Learning to pray is like going on a journey. You are getting to know the One with whom you're traveling, but you don't exactly know the places you will be led.

Prayer can be that kind of adventure.

In the beginning, our prayers are usually simple pleas for help:

"Lord, please watch over my son as he starts school this year."

"Lord, please show me the right answer to this dilemma our family is facing."

"Lord, please give me strength to say and do the right thing in this difficult encounter."

Many who are just starting out in prayer will draw great comfort from using simple written prayers—praying them daily—like my friend who carries the following prayer with him on a card in his pocket:

Almighty God, to You all hearts are open, all desires known, and from You no secrets are hidden. Cleanse the thoughts of my heart by the inspiration of Your Holy Spirit, that I may perfectly love You and worthily magnify Your holy name—through Jesus Christ, our Lord. Amen.[1]

While some men balk at written prayers, my friend says he needs this to help him rededicate himself to personal purity—to remember every day that he belongs fully to God.

Prayers that have been offered by other men, in moments of honest, raw need, can help us express our heart's needs, sometimes better than our own words can. In fact, they can help our own prayer life grow and change and help us find the language of our friendship with Almighty God.

An Invitation From God to Come to Him in Prayer

Some time ago, I encountered an unusual, anonymous writing—written as if to express the Father's own words as He invites us to come to Him. It has, I suppose, undergone many revisions, yet it remains a powerful expression of how God sees us and what He would say to us when we slow down and open our souls to Him in prayer. Though it is long, I want to reproduce it here in total. Read it carefully, and see what aspects of God's heart touch your own.

Come aside and be with me for a while, my son. To please me it is not necessary to know much. All that is required is to love me much, to be deeply sorry for having offended me and desirous of being faithful to me in the future.

Speak to me now as you would to your dearest friend. Tell me all that now fills your mind and heart. Are there any you wish to commend to me? Tell me their names and tell me what you wish me to do for them. Do not fear; ask for much. I love generous hearts which, forgetting themselves, wish well to others.

Speak to me of the poor you wish to comfort. Tell me of the sick that you wish to see relieved. Ask of me something for those who have been unkind to you, or who have crossed you. Ask much for them all. Commend them with all your heart to me.

Ask of me gifts for yourself. Are there not any you would wish to name that would make you happier in yourself, more useful and pleasing to others? Tell me the whole list of favors you want of me. Tell me them with humility, knowing how poor you are without them, how unable you are to gain them by yourself; ask for them with much love, and that they may make you more pleasing to me.

With a child's simplicity, tell me how self-seeking you are. How proud, vain, irritable, how cowardly in sacrifice, how lazy in work, uncertain in your good resolutions. My son, don't run from the sight of so many failings. There are saints in heaven who had the faults you have. They came to me lovingly, they prayed to me earnestly, and my grace has made them good and holy in my sight.

You should be mine, body and soul. Ask of me gifts of body and mind, health, judgment, memory, and success. Ask for them for my sake, that I may be glorified in all things. I can grant everything, and never refuse to give what may make a soul dearer to me and better able to fulfill my will.

Have you no plans for the future which occupy, perhaps distress, your mind? Tell me your hopes, your fears. Is it about your future state? Your position in your work? Or some good you wish to bring to others?

Is it some wish to do good to the souls of others? To some, perhaps, who have ceased to know or care for me? Shall I give you strength, wisdom, and tact to bring these poor ones close to my heart again? Have you failed in the past? Tell me how you acted. I will show why you did not gain all you expected; rely on me, I will help you; and will guide you to lead others to me.

And what crosses do you carry, my son? Are they many, and heavy ones? Has someone caused you pain? Has someone wounded your self-love, and slighted you? Have they injured you? Lay your head upon my shoulder and tell me how you've suffered. Have you felt that some have been ungrateful to you, and unfeeling toward you? Tell me all—and in the warmth of my heart you will find strength to forgive and even to forget that they have ever wished to harm you.

What fears grip you? My providence and protection will comfort you. My love will sustain you. I am never away from you. I can never abandon you. Are friends growing cold in the interest and love they had for you? Pray to me for them. I will restore them to you, if it is good for you and your ability to love and serve me.

Do you have some happiness to make known to me? What's happened since you came to me last, to console you, to gladden and give you joy? What was it? A mark of true friendship you received? A success, unexpected and almost unhoped for? A fear suddenly taken away from you? Did you realize at the same time that it was my will, my love, that brought the thing your heart has so desired? It was my hand, my son, that guided and prepared all for you. Look to me now, my son, and say, "Dear Father, thank you."

You will soon leave me now to go about your day. What promises can you make me? Let them be sincere, humble, full of love and the desire to please me. Tell me how carefully you will avoid the occasions of sin, drive from you all that leads to harm and shun the world's promises, which are empty.

Promise me you will be kind to the poor, loving to friends for my sake, forgiving to your enemies, and charitable to all, not in word alone and action but in your very thoughts. When you have little love for your neighbors, whom you see, you are forgetting me, the one who is hidden from your sight.

Love all my saints. Seek the help of your spiritual friends. I love to glorify them by giving you much through them.

Return to me again soon. Come with your heart empty of the world, for I have more favors to give, more than you can know. Bring your heart so needy that I may fill it with many gifts of my love.

My peace goes with you....

Having read this powerful representation of how the Lord might speak to us in prayer, let's consider some characteristics of true prayer. We'll also see how other men have expressed their hearts to God—and maybe find our voice among theirs.

Honesty

Learning to be completely honest in prayer is as important as being honest in your conversation with your wife, your children, or your closest friends. It's often surprisingly difficult, however, because there seems to be something inside us that wants to use the *right words* when talking with God. *Praying out loud* when you are alone can be a great help. Hearing your words can help you recognize whether or not you're speaking from the heart. Listening to the honest prayers of others—or reading them—can jolt us into reality.

Consider some honest prayers from men of the past. Don't let their lingo throw you. Here is a two-sentence prayer shouted by General Lord Astley (1579-1652) just before entering the Battle of Edgehill:

> *O Lord, Thou knowest how busy I must be this day. And if I forget Thee, do not Thou forget me!*

Or carefully read aloud this prayer written by a conscientious man of God, known only by the name Bernard:

> Lord, I want to love You, yet I'm not sure. I want to trust You, yet I'm afraid of being taken in. I know I need You, yet I'm ashamed of the need. I want to pray, yet I'm afraid of being a hypocrite. I need my independence, yet I fear to be alone. I want to belong, yet I must be myself. Take me, Lord, yet leave me alone. Lord, I believe—help Thou my unbelief. O Lord, if You are there, You do understand, don't You? Give me what I need, but leave me free to choose. Help me work it out my own way, but don't let me go. Let me understand myself, but don't let me despair. Come to me, O Lord—I want You there. Lighten my darkness—but don't dazzle me. Help me to see what I need to do and give me strength to do it.

King David prayed this during a time of intense, honest self-examination:

> Lord, make me to know my end, and what is the measure of my days, that I may know how frail I am (Psalm 39:4, NKJV).

Our heavenly Father would prefer such brief, honest prayers to more formal carefully prepared prayers—as long as they come from our hearts in honesty and humility.

In Need

What loving father does not want his child to come to him seeking help when experiencing a sense of fear or helplessness? The sense of overwhelming smallness, expressed by the anonymous Breton fishermen in the following prayer, reminds me of my smallness when life overwhelms or threatens me:

Dear God, be good to me. The sea is so wide and I am so small.

Early one morning, in prison, just a short time before he was executed by the Nazis, Dietrich Bonhoeffer put pen to paper and recorded a prayer that is remarkable both for its sense of authentic need and at the same time deep peace:

O God, early in the morning I cry to You. Help me to pray and to concentrate my thoughts on You. I cannot do this alone. In me there is darkness, but with You there is light. I am lonely, but You do not leave me. I am feeble in heart, but with You there is help. I am restless, but with You there is peace. In me there is bitterness, but with You there is patience. I do not understand Your ways, but You know the way for me.... Restore me to liberty and enable me so to live now that I may answer before You and before me. Lord, whatever this day may bring, Your name be praised.

Bonhoeffer, a Lutheran pastor and seminary president, had dared to publicly oppose and work for the overthrow of Adolf Hitler and, just like Paul, he spent his last days in prison because he dared to publicly proclaim the Word of God. His sense of total need is combined with a great faith. He shares every conflict of his heart honestly with the Father.

In much the same way, but 400 years earlier, Martin Luther prayed these words out of a deep sense of personal neediness:

Behold, Lord, an empty vessel that needs to be filled. My Lord, fill it. I am weak in the faith. Strengthen me. I am cold in love. Warm me and make me fervent, so that my love may go out to my neighbor. I do not have a strong and firm faith. At times I doubt and am unable to trust You altogether. O Lord, help me. Strengthen my faith and trust in You. In You I have sealed the treasures of all I have. I am poor—but You are rich and did come to be merciful to the poor. I am a sinner—but You are upright. With me there is an abundance of sin—in You is the fullness of righteousness. Therefore, I will remain with You, my God from whom I can receive but to whom I may not give. Amen.

A Kenyan believer expressed his inability to be the man God wanted him to be and prayed a prayer that I often think on:

From the cowardice that dares not face new truth, from the laziness that is contented with half-truth, from the arrogance that thinks it knows all the truth—my good Lord, deliver me!

Asking for Forgiveness

There may be no prayer so precious to God as one in which we realize our failures or sins and humbly ask God's forgiveness. Eloquence does not matter at all here—humility and honesty are all-important. If a man cannot fully acknowledge his own responsibility in sin and failure, he isn't fully a man. And if he cannot come to God openly and ashamed, seeking forgiveness and a changed life, he will not mature—either in this world or in his spiritual walk with God. Consider these words—do you need them?

Dear Father, You know my shame and embarrassment in coming to You at this time. As much as I have affirmed over and over again my desire and determination to be Your man—a wise, patient, and honest man—I have failed You again through _____. I am weak and unfaithful. I do not deserve Your mercy or Your care. But You have promised never to stop loving me. And so I come again to You, and I ask You to have mercy upon me, a sinner. I confess my weakness and my pride and need You to forgive me. Please take away my sin, fill me with Your Holy Spirit and strengthen me to be Your man and to do Your will. I ask this through Him who died and rose again for the sake of sinners like me—Jesus Christ. Amen.

Aaron, the brother of Moses, expressed the way we have felt so often in the following words:

Oh, my Lord! please do not lay this sin on us, in which we have done foolishly and in which we have sinned (Numbers 12:11, NKJV).

We have learned perhaps more from David about asking God's forgiveness than from any other biblical personality:

Have mercy upon me, O God, according to Your loving kindness; according to the multitude of Your tender mercies, blot out my transgressions. Wash me thoroughly from my iniquity, and cleanse me from my sin. For I acknowledge my transgressions, and my sin is ever before me. Against You, You only, have I sinned, and done this evil in Your sight ... Create in me a clean heart, O God, and renew a steadfast spirit within me (Psalm 51:1-4, 10, NKJV).

Over and over David fell into sin—only to come back to his Father in heaven in humility with words such as these:

Turn Yourself to me, and have mercy on me, for I am desolate and afflicted. The troubles of my heart have enlarged; Oh, bring me out of my distresses! Look on my affliction and my pain (Psalm 25:16-18, NKJV).

Personal Dedication

For each of us, as men, there are times when we know we need to step up to the plate and make a significant, new commitment to God and to His purposes. These are holy moments, times in which something deeper happens. One such moment came for a man named Charles deFoucauld about a century ago. He prayed:

> My Father, I abandon myself to You. Do with me as You will. Whatever You may do with me, I thank You. I am prepared for anything, I accept everything. Provided Your will is fulfilled in me and in all creatures, I ask for nothing more, my God. I place my soul in Your hands. I give it to You, my God, with all the love of my heart because I love You. And for me it is a necessity of love, this gift of myself—so I place myself in Your hands without reserve, in boundless confidence, because You are my Father.

A man who brings himself to God in this way is a man who can expect God to bring into his life *goodness, challenge, growth,* and *a lifetime of meaning and fulfillment.*

Similarly, the following prayer of commitment expresses a yielding of personal ambition, an intensity of devotion to God—both of which speak of making a major step forward in personal discipleship. In a real sense, this is a once-in-a-lifetime prayer, not to be repeated. But the substance of it is something we reaffirm regularly:

> I am no longer my own, but Yours. Put me to what You will, rank me with whom You will. Put me to doing. Put me to suffering. Let me be

employed for You, or laid aside for You. Exalted for You, or brought low for You. Let me be full, let me be empty. Let me have all things, let me have nothing. I freely and heartily yield all things to Your pleasure and disposal. And now, O glorious and blessed God, Father, Son, and Holy Spirit, You are mine and I am Yours. So be it. And the covenant which I have made on earth—let it be ratified in heaven! (Methodist Covenant Service)

Every day we can express our desire and determination to be God's man in the spirit of this simple prayer from an ancient English prayer book:

God be in my head, and in my understanding. God be in my eyes, and in my looking. God be in my mouth, and in my speaking. God be in my heart, and in my thinking. God be at my end, and at my departing. (Old Sarum Primer)

Again, David expressed the same sentiments in the familiar words:

Search me, O God, and know my heart; try me, and know my anxieties; and see if there is any wicked way in me, and lead me in the way everlasting (Psalm 139:23-24, NKJV).

All prayer is precious to God, but prayers such as these seem to me particularly holy because of the spirit of submission that permeates them.

These sort of prayers are always answered by God with a resounding *yes!* And as we mature in our heart-to-heart relationship with God, we eventually come to a place where we learn that even when some of our prayers are wrongly motivated, or foolishly mistaken in their sentiments, God's answer is always the answer of love. Even when God says *no*, it is a loving no from an all-wise Father in heaven. And you can join the one, now long gone, who penned the following:

> *I asked for strength that I might achieve; I was made weak that I might learn humbly to obey. I asked for health that I might do greater things; I was given infirmity that I might do better things. I asked for riches that I might be happy; I was given poverty that I might be wise. I asked for power that I might have the praise of men; I was given weakness that I might feel the need of God. I asked for all things that I might enjoy life; I was given life that I might enjoy all things. I got nothing that I had asked for, but everything that I had hoped for. Almost despite myself my unspoken prayers were answered; I am, among all men, most richly blessed.* (Prayer of an unknown Confederate soldier)

Give yourself to God in prayer. Pray regularly. Honestly. Humbly. Persistently. Focus on God the Father, His Son Jesus Christ, and the Holy Spirit rather than on your own faith or lack of it.

When you pray in this way, I can assure you, God *will* hear you! He will honor your concerns for your wife and children and all that concerns you. And He will *answer* you—in *His* time.

God will never fail, and the man who prays knows this to be true—and best of all, he knows God himself.

If you have never committed your whole life—body, soul, ambitions, and well-being—to God, *do it now*.

And then set out on the adventurous journey of prayer. Your family, for generations to come, will know the difference because of your life. Isn't that what you want?

For Thought and Discussion

1. Can you recall and describe a time in which God did not give you what you asked for and you eventually realized that this was an example of God's "love no," that not getting what you requested was for the best?

2. Do you generally remember to pray at the outset or in the midst of a particularly challenging or difficult situation? Or do you forget? What could be some benefits of praying sooner than later?

3. Consider the following types of prayer and decide which is easiest for you and which is hardest:

   ◆ Thanking God

   ◆ Expressing your needs to God, asking His help in specific situations

   ◆ Telling God honestly how you are doing, what you are thinking and feeling

   ◆ Interceding on behalf of others

   ◆ Confessing specific sin and accepting forgiveness

   ◆ Dedicating yourself or committing yourself completely— mind, body, and soul

   Why is your hardest choice difficult for you? Why is your easiest easy? Does this tell you anything about yourself or about your own personal view of God?

3. Perhaps it would be wise to look back through this book and note the passages, concepts, and suggestions that you marked and then, reflecting upon them, ask yourself, "How do I want to grow in my prayer life?" You may want to share your answer with another person who will pray for *you* in these areas.

Note:
1. Some of the prayers in this chapter are simply prayers that I have collected from various sources. Others are from our own Episcopal church *Book of Common Prayer* (Church Hymnal Corp., 800 Second Ave., New York, NY 10012). Some are taken from George Appleton, General Editor, *Oxford Book of Prayer* (New York: Oxford University Press, 1985).

Shape your Child's Heart through Prayer

Nurture, model , encourage, and guide your children through everyday life by praying specifically, and discover:

- ◆ 12 important character traits
- ◆ life-changing transformations
- ◆ fun, practical activities

while they were sleeping

12 character traits for moms to pray

anne arkins & gary harrell

Connect with your children through prayer and transform their young lives for a lifetime!

Item #8236

$9.99

FAMILYLIFE . . .
the leader in Marriage Conference